Write It Right!

Write It Right!

A Guide for Clear and Correct Writing

RICHARD ANDERSEN and HELENE HINIS

SkillPath Publications
Mission, Kansas

ISBN: 1-878542-30-3

Editor: Kelly Scanlon

ACKNOWLEDGMENTS: No book is the product of a single person and *Write It Right!* had the help of many, most notably Chris Abiera, Denise Dudley, Randy Hermance, Carolyn Martin, and Kelly Scanlon.

Printed in the United States of America

For Ourania Hinis

CONTENTS

CONTENTS

Discovering Your Writing Voice

HOW TO DEVELOP A STYLE OF YOUR OWN

Style is what identifies you as you. It's the way you walk, the way you dress, the way you say what you have to say. It's your badge of who you are.

In the same way that your clothes reflect your personality, so too should your writing style. Have you ever called someone you know on the telephone and, before you could identify yourself, the person you were speaking to recognized your voice and said your name? That's because you have an individual speaking voice that separates you from everyone else. That speaking voice—the words and phrases that you use—is as unique and distinct as your fingerprints.

You also have an individual writing voice that separates you from everyone else, but because of the way you were taught to write, you were never given the opportunity to develop it. In fact, you were never taught how to write; you were taught how to edit.

Remember the first writing book you ever had? Remember all those lessons on nouns and pronouns? Remember the hours you spent diagramming sentences?

That wasn't writing. That was editing.

And what happened the first time you did get a chance to write?

To say your teacher "edited" what you wrote is the polite word for what your teacher did.

And it didn't take you very long to realize that no matter how hard you tried, no matter how good your writing was, your teacher could always find something wrong with it.

And the next year's teacher wasn't much different. And neither was your first boss. And neither is your present boss. And your future boss won't be either.

This constant criticism of your writing by those who have power over you has undermined your confidence in your writing ability.

So how are you handling it? The same way you always have: by copying other people's words, phrases, and sentence structures—the few that haven't been attacked with blood-red ink—and passing them off as your own.

And you're not alone. Why else do you think so many memos and letters read:

- In reference to your letter of . . .
- As per your request for . . .
- Pursuant to our telephone conversation . . .
- Enclosed herewith please find . . .

If you want to become a lively, effective, and engaging writer, then starting today, you have to:

Write in your own voice.

And how do you do that? By writing as closely as possible to the way you speak. The closer you can get your writing voice to the way you speak, the more lively, powerful, and engaging your writing will be.

Now, when we say to write the way you speak, we don't mean you should write *exactly* the way you speak. There are things you do when you speak that you can't do when you write. For example, you could never write this in the third paragraph of a business letter: "Look, Joe, you know what I said in that first paragraph? Forget it. I've changed my mind."

That kind of writing has no place in a business letter.

When we say you should write in your own voice, we mean you should write in the speaking voice that's most appropriate for the person you're writing to. One example of a speaking voice that is also a good model for your writing voice is the voice you use when you speak on the telephone. When you talk to clients, customers, or colleagues on the telephone, you don't use slang or the idiomatic expressions you use when speaking to members of your family or to your friends. The voice you use on the telephone is natural.

It's also professional. You've learned through experience what to say and what not to say. You've learned which words work and which words don't. You've learned which words bring about one reaction from your listeners and which words bring about another.

So why not use the words you've tested on the phone?

When your telephone rings at work, do you like to hear from the person who's cold and impersonal and gets right down to business, or do you like to hear from the person who asks how you are and talks with you about *you* before bringing up the reason for the call?

You'd probably rather hear from the second caller. The same is true for your readers. They want to hear from the person they spoke with on the phone. So give them that same natural voice you use on the phone—the one they're used to. It will improve the quality of your writing and, at the same time, maintain the professional standards expected in a business letter or memo.

And your boss will be happy too. Here's why:

> **We speak in simple, clear, easy-to-understand sentences. When we write like we speak, our messages are simple, clear, and easy to understand.**

No boss ever complained, "Hold on here a minute; this sentence is way too clear."

But there are bosses who confuse clear writing with a mistaken idea of professional writing.

Compare this paragraph of "professional" writing:

> Operationally, teaching effectiveness is measured by assessing the levels of agreement between the perceptions of instructors and students on the rated ability of specific instructional behavior attributes which were employed during the course instruction.

with what Tom Watson—past chair of the Executive Committee at IBM—
has to say:

> TO ALL IBM MANAGERS:
>
> A foreign language has been creeping into many of the presenta-
> tions I hear and the memos I read. It adds nothing to a message
> but noise, and I want your help in stamping it out.
>
> It's called "gobbledygook."
>
> There's no shortage of examples. Nothing seems to get done
> anymore; everything gets "finalized." Things don't happen at the
> same time but "coincident with this action." Believe it or not,
> people will talk about taking a "commitment position" and then,
> because of the "volatility of schedule changes," they will
> "decommit," so that our "posture" will be able to "enhance
> competitive positions."
>
> This is gobbledygook.
>
> It may be acceptable among bureaucrats, but not in this com-
> pany. IBM wasn't built with fuzzy ideas and pretentious language.
> IBM was built with clear thinking and plain talk. Let's keep it that
> way.

No problem! But what do you do if you have a boss who hasn't read
Watson's memo and thinks muddled writing is a sign of intelligence?

Still write every assignment in your own voice.

That will give you the opportunity to discover and develop your own natural writing style. Then, once your words are on the paper:

Edit what you've written into the voice your boss approves of.

You'll discover that writing in your own voice first and then editing into your boss's voice once the words are on paper is a lot faster and easier than trying to edit the two voices in your mind. You'll also come a lot closer to representing the voice your boss approves of. But don't be surprised or discouraged or depressed if, after you've given your boss what he or she wants, your boss still makes changes. Bosses do this for two reasons: they think it's their responsibility (read: if they don't make changes, they're not doing their job) OR they take pleasure in it (read: they like the power of making other people think their work is never good enough).

Most of the time these bosses are not correcting mistakes; most of the time they're changing preferences in style. But because of the way we were taught to write, we assume the changes are to correct mistakes, and we feel diminished.

So what can we do?

Don't take any editing personally.

It's not you; it's them. How many times have you written something, sent it to someone for approval, made that person's corrections, sent it to some-one else, incorporated that person's corrections, sent it to a third person, and seen it come back the same way you wrote it in the first place? How many of your bosses have mistaken their own corrections for your writing and then corrected their own corrections?

Don't give your boss the final draft.

Give your boss the next-to-final draft. And triple-space it. This changes the dynamics of the relationship between you and your boss. Your relationship now goes from "Okay, here's the best I can do. Now go ahead—dump on me" to "Here's the next-to-final draft of your letter; make whatever changes you want. Let's work on this together. Let's make this the best letter the two of us can possibly produce."

You can then incorporate your boss's changes into the final draft and submit it for his or her approval or signature. By using this approach, you not only get to discover and develop your own natural writing voice, you also get to protect it from bosses who make changes. And you'll discover that after a few months, your boss will stop making changes in the next-to-final drafts. Why? Because it's no fun to make changes in the next-to-final draft! It's only fun to make changes in the one you've worked hardest on and is printed on the best paper in the office. And as your boss makes fewer and fewer changes, he or she will come to respect you more and more as a writer and as a worker.

HOW TO MAKE YOUR STYLE PROFESSIONAL

The things that make a memo good and the things that make a novel good—in terms of the writing—are the same. The principles of good writing stay the same; only the format changes. If you write as closely as possible to the way you speak, everything you write will be simple and clear and easy to understand. Everything you write will contain all the principles of good writing and set you apart from the insecure writers whose memos and letters sound so much alike.

As much as your writing will improve, however, there are still a few things you can do to make it better, to fine-tune those basic principles, to make your individual memos and letters not only well written but powerful and effective as well.

This is where editing comes in. Many people think real writers—those who make their living as writers—have an enormous pool of talent and everything they write comes out perfect with the first draft. While it is true that writers with talent (read: those who've discovered their own voices) can occasionally come close to perfection with a first draft, they know that editing and proofreading is what makes the difference between engaging prose and art.

Although both editing and proofreading are concerned with details such as correct spelling and grammar, editing is concerned with a much bigger picture. When you edit, you first look at a piece of writing from the point of view of content and tone. Then you analyze the paragraphs, looking for whether they vary in length and whether you've developed the topic. Then you examine each sentence for structure, grammar, and syntax. Finally, you study each word, asking yourself whether it's spelled correctly and whether it's the best word for communicating your message.

Once a piece of writing has been edited, it is given a final reading, or proof-reading, to ensure that *everything* is correct. Proofreading is concerned more with the fine details of mechanics: spelling, punctuation, overall appearance, consistency in style, and so forth.

Here are some easy tips for editing and proofreading your memos and letters:

**Put some time and distance between
what you write and what you edit.**

Have you ever written a really important letter—one in which there could be no mistakes—and then proofread that letter word for word, maybe even three or four times, to make sure you did everything right? Then, a week or so later, you saw a copy of that letter and noticed some stupid, little mistake that you'd never made in your whole life, but now when it was so important to be correct, you made the credibility-killing blunder?

Happens a lot.

The reason is that the letter was so important. Because it was so important, you began proofreading soon after you finished writing it. When you proofread right after you've written something, two things happen:

- *Your mind goes into "cheerleader mode."* You're reading what you've written, and your mind is telling you "Great! Terrific! Fantastic! Mail it!" If you've ever written something you thought was first-rate, then seen it a week later and thought, "How could I think this was so good?" you know what the Cheerleader Voice sounds like.

- *Your eyes correct without telling you.* Your eyes have an uncanny ability to come across a misspelled or misused word and literally correct that word without telling you. Your eyes will see the *there* you meant to write when you wrote *their*; they will even fill in a word that you left out of a sentence. And they won't always let you know about it.

So, put some time and distance between what you write and what you edit. The more time and distance you put between what you write and what you edit, the more objective you'll be, the more mistakes you'll find, the better the job of editing you'll do. Consider doing all of your writing before lunch and all of your editing after lunch. Consider doing all of your writing one day and all of your editing the next. And, when it comes time to edit, consider editing at some place other than where you wrote your first draft. If you write at a computer terminal, consider editing from a printout or perhaps turning your terminal around and sitting on the other side of your desk. These seemingly small things can make a big difference.

Here's why: When we write, we focus on *what* we want to say; when we edit, we focus on *how* we've said it. Changing physical positions helps us take off our writer's hat and put on our editor's hat.

Edit every memo and letter three times.

After you've come back from that break you've put between your writing and the editing, pick up what you've written, sit back in your chair, and read your memo or letter the way your reader would. Generally. This first read is known as:

Editing for meaning. All you want to do at this point is make sure that what you've written is simple, clear, and easy to understand. Put yourself in the reader's place. Ask yourself whether you've given the reader enough information. Is it obvious to the reader what you want done, when you want it done by, and what you may do for the reader if he or she can get it done on time?

After you're sure your reader will have no difficulty understanding your message, you're ready to read the memo or letter a second time. This is called:

Editing for power. Here's where you take your message to a higher level. Ask yourself:

- Does my opening sentence grab the reader's attention? Is it short, simple, and clear? Does it have to be read only once to be understood? Is there something in my opening sentence that my reader can relate to in a personal way? Does my opening sentence raise my reader's curiosity and make him or her want to read on?

- Are any of my paragraphs or sentences too long? The more complicated the subject, the shorter your paragraphs and sentences should be. Beware, however, of winding up with too many short sentences in a row. The choppiness will distract your reader from the message.

- Does each point lead to the next? Is each sentence a stepping stone for the one that comes after it?

- How about the words? Can I replace any jargon (words such as *prioritize* and *optimize* and *interface*) or clichés ("As per your request . . ." "Enclosed please find . . .")? Can I replace any long words with shorter ones? The bigger the word, the more opportunities there are to make a spelling mistake. Abraham Lincoln's Gettysburg Address has 257 words; 196 of them are only one syllable long.

Although you will have found most of your spelling, punctuation, and grammatical errors by the end of your second read, you want to read your memo or letter again, this time focusing only on whatever mechanical errors you may have missed. This is known as:

Editing for correctness. If your letters contain mistakes, your readers will think that either you don't know better or you don't care enough to correct mistakes. Or both. To avoid these reactions, ask yourself:

- Is the date right?

- Have I correctly spelled the name of my reader and the name of his or her company? If you spell these names incorrectly—and don't take the spelling of any name for granted—then you have to win back a reader who hasn't yet read the first word of your message.

- Is my message free of all spelling, punctuation, and grammatical errors? Have I been consistent in my choices of what I think is correct?

If you're not sure whether something you've written is correct, then read the whole sentence aloud.
If you're still not sure, then read it to someone else.

Your eyes can easily be deceived. But not your ears. If you've written something and you're not sure whether it's right, just read the sentence aloud. Your ears will tell you immediately whether what you've written is correct. If, however, you're still not sure, read what you've written to someone else. Whatever answer you get will be correct 100 percent of the time. Your listener may not be able to tell you exactly what's wrong with your sentence, but he or she will be able to tell just by listening whether it's correctly written.

Now that you've edited your writing, you're ready to type up a final copy that includes all the changes or corrections you made during the editing stage. Once you have this final copy, you need to *proofread* it to make sure you made all the changes you intended to make and to ensure that you didn't introduce any typos or other errors into the copy when you made your changes. The proofreading stage also gives you one final opportunity to spot any misspellings or punctuation errors.

There are three main ways to proofread: solo proofreading, team proofreading, and computer proofreading.

1. *Solo proofreading.* Solo proofreading involves reading your piece of writing yourself, preferably against the copy that contains all your editorial changes. There are four main steps to solo proofreading:

   - Read your final copy against the copy you used to make all of your editorial changes. Read it word for word, punctuation mark for punctuation mark. Comparing your edited version to your final version in this way ensures that you actually picked up all the changes you intended to.

   - Next take a blank piece of paper and cover all the lines of your memo or letter except the last. Then read the last line backwards from right to left. When you reach the left-hand margin, move your blank piece of paper up to the next line and repeat the process all the way to the top line of your memo or letter.

   - Then reverse the process. Put your blank piece of paper over all the lines in your memo or letter except the top line. Read the top line from left to right the way you normally would. But don't move your blank piece of paper to the next line until your eyes have reached the right-hand margin.

   After following this practice, you'll notice that on your way up the memo or letter, you will discover all your misspelled words and typographical errors. Going down the memo or letter, you will notice all your misused words (the time you wrote *their* when you meant to write *there*) as well as any words you may have left out. You'll also catch the words that were formed when you left letters out and your computer's spellcheck system didn't notice. Like the time you wrote about how you were going to increase the company's assets, left the "t" out of "assets," and felt exactly like what you were going to work so hard on increasing.

- Check the trouble spots. Zero in, one final time, on commas, periods, capital letters, underlines and boldface type, quotation marks, apostrophes, numbers, headings, and any areas that you know give you particular trouble.

- Read your memo or letter again from beginning to end.

2. *Team proofreading.* Team proofreading requires two people. One person reads aloud from the edited copy while the second person follows on the final copy. The reader must be sure to read not only every word but also every piece of punctuation and every paragraph break.

3. *Computer proofreading.* Most word processing packages come with a program that checks your document for correct spelling. Some even have programs that check your grammar. Although these programs are useful for finding some of your more obvious mistakes, you should not rely solely on them to catch all of your mistakes. Here are some of the errors these programs routinely miss:

- Words that have more than one spelling. A spelling checker will not alert you to *hear* when you meant to write *here.*

- Words that you don't type but should have.

- Words that you should have capitalized but didn't and vice versa.

- Words that are improperly hyphenated. If you use your computer's automatic hyphenation program, it may not hyphenate some words correctly. For example, the word *present* could be hyphenated "pres-ent" or "pre-sent," depending on whether you're using it as a noun or as a verb.

- Words that you type twice. If you type the word *and* twice in a row, some computer spelling programs will not alert you. Some of the more sophisticated ones will, however.

Editor's Checklist

Content
- Is it complete?
- Is it accurate?

Tone
- Appropriate: for writer's goal?
               for reader's attitude?
- Personal?

Paragraphs
- Vary in length?
- One major topic in each?
- Flow together coherently?
- Sentences flow logically?

Sentences
- Vary in length?
- Only one major idea in each?

Words
- Have I replaced each word that is unnecessarily large, obscure, or overused with one that is short, common, or clear?
- Have I used the passive voice judiciously?
- Do the words express the meaning I'm trying to convey?
- Will the reader be able to FEEL my message?

The Reader's First Impression
- Is the stationery attractive and clean?
- Do I address the reader by name?
- Is the name spelled correctly?
- Are the margins even?
- Is all tabular matter in line?
- Is the print dark and even?
- Have I used headings or white space to help the reader focus his or her attention?

Proofreading Checklist

- **Eliminate distractions.**

- **Gather the proper tools.**

- **Separate yourself from the writing.**

- **Remember the goal of the communication.**

- **Read the document backwards, word for word.**

- **Check the trouble spots:**
  - Commas
  - Periods
  - Capital Letters
  - Underlines/Boldface
  - Quotation Marks
  - Apostrophes
  - Numbers
  - Headings
  - Others

- **Read the document through for meaning.**

Eight Proofreading Symbols

DELETE

cheeck   ofwfice   Mrr.   editting

ADD

chck   ofice   M.   editng

TRANSPOSE

chceek   ofifce   M.r   ediitng

MAKE LOWERCASE

cheCk   oFfice   MR.   EdiTing

MAKE UPPERCASE

Skillpath   mr.   new York   buddha

CLOSE UP SPACE

Skill Path   of fice   Mr .   edit ing

ADD SPACE

NewYork   officebuilding   Mr.Jones   BillyJoel

NEW PARAGRAPH

The managers who attended last week's meeting were satisfied with Jack's report.　Next week, we will discuss three new topics.

CHAPTER 2

The Writer-Editor Relationship

HOW TO EDIT WRITERS AND NOT BE CALLED A "BUTCHER"

Editing writers is not changing their writing to the way you would say the same thing—even when you think your way is best. Editing writers is helping them say what they want to say. General guideline for editors: *If it's not wrong, don't change it.*

That having been said, we should also note that every writer needs a good editor. Writers appreciate when their mistakes are corrected—that saves them from embarrassment and makes them look good to their readers—but they bristle when someone with power makes a change that they don't see as an improvement. Here's how you can improve your writers' ability to communicate effectively, build their confidence, make less work for yourself, and see that any suggestions you may make are not only appreciated but sought.

Give your writers a chance to say what they have to say.

Read the writer's memo or letter all the way to the end before making any corrections. How many times have you started correcting a piece of writing only to have to go back and erase your corrections because you discovered that your questions were answered later? Or how many times have you made corrections thinking your writer was going in one direction only to discover that he or she was taking you in another? Give your writers a chance to say what they have to say. Then, if you're still confused, give the memo or letter back to the writer. Tell the writer in specific terms what confuses you. Notes such as "vague" and "unclear" don't mean anything to most writers. What specifically isn't clear? What does this sentence really say? How can the writer's message be misinterpreted? After telling the writer in specific terms where the confusion arises, ask the writer to make the necessary changes.

When you make changes without consulting the writer, you undermine the writer's confidence. The writer begins to feel that no matter how hard the effort, no matter how good the writing, you'll always find something wrong with it. So why, the writer asks, should I try? Once the writer asks that question, your work load starts to double. Over time, it can triple and even quadruple.

One of the toughest jobs of being an editor is putting your ego in your pocket and allowing a writer's phrase to stand in place of your own. If, however, you believe your phrase really will make a difference to the reader, ask the writer to consider both phrases. When you let the writer choose, you show that you have confidence in the writer's ability, you avoid stepping unnecessarily and in crippling ways on the writer's toes, you begin developing a good rapport with the writer, and you make it possible for the writer to see your suggestions as power aids rather than power plays.

Analyze what the writer has written.

Not every memo or letter needs to be improved. Not every memo or letter requires a change. Sometimes, you can do a better job of editing by not making any changes. Or at least by restricting your changes to those that are necessary.

To analyze any memo or letter, read it three times, moving from the general to the particular. The first time through, ask yourself:

- *Is the message clear?* What is the point of this memo or letter? Generally, the sooner the writer gets to the point the better. Once the writer has made his or her point, does he or she stick to it? Is the point developed in a coherent way? Is there anything that might distract the reader from the point the writer is trying to make?

- *Is the message accessible?* Even if the subject is complex, it should be easy to read. No sentence should have to be read twice in order to be understood. Nor should any sentence have to be waded through. How many times have you read up to the first comma in a sentence, stopped to figure out what the writer said, then moved on to the second comma, translated, and so on until you finally reached a period and could breathe a sigh of relief and collect your thoughts?

- *Are there any unnecessary words?* Most writers work so hard at getting their words on paper that they have almost as hard a time removing any of them. You know that the more words you can get rid of in any memo or letter, the more power and energy you preserve, but writers can't always see how any of the words they've labored over for so long could possibly be counterproductive. So rather than remove their words for them, try to show your writers how a message can be improved by leaving words out. Read a wordy sentence aloud to your writer, once with all the words in and once with the unnecessary words left out. Then ask your writer to do the same with any other wordy sentences. It's important for the writer to make as many of his or her own changes as possible. The time you spend early showing your writers how to do this will save you much more time later.

Listen to what your writers tell you.

The basis of good editing is a good relationship with your writer. So make personal rather than professional your first response to any written work. Say something good about how your writer's opinion or idea makes you feel. Show that you value your writer's thoughts and insights.

Then, as hard as it may be, listen. Because of the power editors have, they often do most of the talking in any conference with a writer. But telling a writer what he or she did wrong doesn't help. It only undermines the writer's confidence. And you don't want that. You want your writers to discover and correct their own problems. Ask your writers the kinds of open-ended questions that will get them talking: What did you like about what you wrote? Do you have any plans for another draft? What did you learn from working on this assignment?

Once you have your writers talking, you can ask the questions that will help them discover what they need to know. This process may initially take more time than just correcting their mistakes, but it will save you more than just time in the future. It will save you the energy needed to deal with the many ways unhappy writers can torment their editors. Think, for example, of the problems you'd face if you had to work with a writer who'd become indifferent to his or her work.

Finally, ask your writers questions like "What questions would you like to ask me?" or "What can I do to help you?" Do not ask questions like "Any questions?" "Any questions?" means "I'm only asking 'Any questions?' because I should, not because I expect to answer any." It has the same effect as ending a letter with "If you have any questions, please call me." Readers know you don't really want to hear from them. You either don't know a better way to end your letter or are too lazy to think of one.

And when you answer your writers' questions, don't be negative. Instead of saying "This isn't right," try asking "What do you think about ordering your words this way?" Instead of telling writers that their work is bad, wrong, or incorrect, try to get the writer to think of his or her work in terms of what is effective or ineffective. Writers will discover more workable solutions to their problems if they learn to ask "What works best in this particular situation with this particular reader?" instead of "What's the correct thing to do?"

A Final Word for Editors

Don't call any writer a "hack."

You'll do a much better job as an editor if instead of correcting every mistake your writers make, you can convince them you are on their side. To establish this level of trust, your writers must be certain of your confidence in them as writers.

Once your writers learn to trust you, they will want to do more of your work for you. They will see it as their own and take pride in what they accomplish. Without this trust, your writers will see their work as never being good enough and think of you as a "butcher" who knows something about writing but understands little about anything else.

HOW TO WRITE FOR EDITORS AND NOT BE CALLED A "HACK"

Although they may not seem like it, editors are human beings too. They have the same fears and insecurities as writers and want to do just as good a job. The problem is, they think differently. Whereas you're concerned with *what* you want to say, editors focus on *how* you've said it.

Here are some ways to improve your relationship with your editor:

Talk before you write.

Find out what your editor thinks is most important in any assignment. Make your questions as specific as possible. Don't wait for your editor to volunteer information he or she probably hasn't thought of yet. When the ideas start coming, keep them flowing. The more information you gather, the easier your writing will be. And don't be afraid to ask for advice. It's the one thing editors love to give.

Listen before you think.

No writer knows it all. Be open to suggestions; be willing to take criticism; be agreeable to different kinds of writing assignments. Listen to what your editors have to say as if it were all true. And keep those reactions coming. On the other hand, don't be tyrannized by any editor. Don't write anything you don't believe in. Editors may always be right because they have the power, but they come attached to their own set of blinders and may not always understand your perspective. Editors, as much as writers, need to be told when one of their suggestions isn't justified.

Support before you criticize.

Help your editor by getting your work done on time. Editors have schedules too, and the more time you give them between your assignment and their deadline, the more time, energy, and interest they'll have to help you improve as a writer. Build your editor's confidence in you by proofreading carefully and making sure all your facts are accurate.

Question before you challenge.

Editors appreciate good writers as much as writers appreciate good editors. Give editors the feedback they need, but do it gently. Editors have feelings too. When they say something you wrote is "awful," they really mean it didn't work for them. It still could be pretty good. In fact, some of the best pieces of writing are hated by most people. So don't look to your editors to find out whether what you've written is good. Look instead to discover how your particular words make other people respond. Then *you* decide whether your words are any good.

A Final Word To Writers

Don't call any editor a "butcher."

Editing means making what you said as clear as possible to your readers. It means finding the most effective structure and words and throwing away the rest. If you have to make introductions or transitions, you have things in the wrong order. If you retain words that aren't essential, you sap your reader's strength. Every word you eliminate keeps your reader with you for one more sentence. So cut the fat; get to the heart of the matter. Experience the pleasure and power of the scalpel. Editing is a positive, creative, life-giving act. When you edit your work well, you save time and energy for your editor and win his or her trust and confidence in return.

CHAPTER

3

Composition

PARAGRAPHS

PARAGRAPHS WERE INVENTED BY THE GREEKS WHO DIDN'T HAVE PUNCTUATION MARKS AND WROTE EVERY SENTENCE THE WAY YOU'RE READING THIS ONLY IT WAS WORSE BECAUSE NOT ONLY WERE ALL THE LETTERS CAPITALIZED THERE WERE NO SPACES BETWEEN THE WORDS EACH LONG UNBROKEN PIECE OF HAND-WRITING WAS CALLED A <u>PARA</u> AND IT QUICKLY TIRED THE EYES AND MINDS OF MANY A GREEK WHO HAD TO WORK TO FIGURE OUT WHERE ONE THOUGHT ENDED AND ANOTHER BEGAN SO THE GREEKS CREATED THIS LITTLE SYMBOL CALLED A <u>GRAPHO</u> TO PUT IN THE MARGINS OF THEIR <u>PARAS</u> WHENEVER THE GREEKS CAME TO A <u>GRAPHO</u> THEY COULD PUT A FINGER ON IT AND REST THEIR EYES AND MINDS WITHOUT LOSING THEIR PLACE TODAY'S EDITORS USE THE SAME MARK TO TELL WRITERS AT WHAT POINT TO BEGIN A NEW <u>PARAGRAPH</u> HERE'S WHAT IT LOOKS LIKE:

¶

25

Paragraphs today are still visual signals. They tell you that you no longer have to mark your rest stop with your finger. Now you can stop, give your eyes a rest, breathe a little more deeply, and collect your thoughts before going on to the next paragraph. Here are some guidelines to help you write clear, easy-to-understand, effective paragraphs:

Limit every paragraph to one topic.

Stick to one topic for each paragraph and your messages will be easily accessible to your readers, who'll also appreciate the opportunities you give them to rest their eyes and minds.

Vary the length of your paragraphs.

There are no limits on how long a paragraph should be, but varying the length of your paragraphs is one way to keep your readers engaged in what you have to say. Short paragraphs—one word or one sentence long—attract your readers' attention all by themselves and are good for stating the points you want to make. Explanatory paragraphs demand a longer length. The key is variety. You want some long paragraphs, some short, and some in-between. Make sure, however, that none of your paragraph breaks seem forced or artificial.

Open each paragraph with your main idea.

Stating the main idea upfront is the fastest and easiest way to engage your readers because your main idea is the most important thing you have to say. It's also what your readers want to learn first. Sometimes, however, you may want to leave the best for last. Sometimes you may want to build up to something so the effect on your readers is similar to the punch line of a joke. Both are effective techniques as long as you have an opening sentence that carries your readers through to the line that waits for them at the end. Most of the time, however, you want to get to the point of your paragraph right in the very first line.

Develop your paragraphs.

We've been told that a paragraph is a single idea, but we've also been told that a sentence is a single idea. And so's a word. If words, sentences, and paragraphs are all single ideas, how do we develop a paragraph beyond a word or a sentence? Here are some ways to develop paragraphs:

- *Give specific examples of what you're writing about.* Don't just write "Mary remains calm under pressure." Tell of the time the report was due and how Mary reacted when she discovered no one had begun writing it.

- *Support your statements with proof, and present it in ways the reader can understand and appreciate.* Don't just say that "Americans should read more"; call attention to a source that reveals that 60 percent of America's families didn't buy a book last year.

- *Use quotations or paraphrases to cite what others have to say.* Don't just tell your readers "It's important to omit unnecessary words"; summon Peter DeVries to announce "When I see a paragraph shrinking under my pen like bacon on a skillet, I know I'm going in the right direction."

Here are some ways to present the information you use to develop your paragraphs:

- *Start with the general and move toward the specific.* When you begin a paragraph with a statement such as "The company's sales performance was outstanding this year," you're making a general statement. Present statistics or other information by sales category to specifically explain what you mean by "outstanding."

- *Move from the specific to the general.* Using the previous example of sales, you could begin your paragraph with a sentence such as "Sales of lipstick increased by 22 percent over last year's figures, and the new line of mascara earned revenues that exceeded estimates by 8.5 percent." Other sentences in that paragraph could lead to a general conclusion that "Overall, the company's sales performance was outstanding this year."

- *Present information according to time sequence.* There are two ways to do this. One way is to list the information in the order it happened, from beginning to end. The other way is to reverse the order of the events, first starting with what happened last and then describing the events that led up to it.

- *Compare and contrast ideas.* Present the pros and cons of a situation or an idea and then come to a conclusion or develop a recommendation.

Make your paragraphs follow a logical progression.

Your paragraphs should lead your readers from one point to the next. Each paragraph should plant a thought in your readers' minds, and the following paragraphs should develop that thought. When you successfully plant the main thought of your paragraph in your readers' minds, you eliminate most of the need for transitions. You allow your readers to make the leap from one paragraph to the next in their imaginations.

- *The opening paragraph.* Your opening paragraph introduces the idea being considered. Remember, in the opening paragraph, you're making your first impression on your readers. If you don't grab their attention immediately, they may not carefully read what you have to say—or they may not read it at all! Use the first paragraph to ask a question, state an opinion, or give a brief but lively description of the issue to be discussed. Engage your readers!

- *The middle paragraphs.* Your middle paragraphs support or clarify the topic you introduced in your first paragraph. If a paragraph doesn't add to the idea under discussion, take it out—it will only muddle your message. Along the same line, get rid of any paragraphs that simply restate ideas you've already presented.

Another way to distract readers is to wander from the point you're trying to make. All of your sentences should focus on one idea. Get rid of any sentences that don't promote your main idea, or use them in another paragraph to develop another idea.

Finally, paragraphs that raise more questions than they answer not only reflect poorly on you as a writer but also can create plenty of office headaches. Imagine writing a memo that states a new company policy, but either leaving out critical information or only alluding to parts of the policy. Now imagine all the phone calls you're going to get from employees who want clarification!

- *The final paragraph.* The last paragraph often brings together all of your ideas or restates your major points. This is your opportunity to draw a conclusion, make recommendations or suggestions, or summarize your ideas. Above all, avoid a closing paragraph that is full of meaningless clichés or that brings up a new topic.

SENTENCES

Sentences can be simple, compound, complex, compound-complex, cumulative, short, long, periodic, declarative, interrogative, exclamatory, mixed, fragmented, and fused. But there's only one bottom line for every sentence:

Clarity.

If your readers don't understand what you're trying to say, the whole sentence is a failure. And no amount of punctuation will save a poorly written sentence. The fastest, easiest, and most effective ways to write clear, easy-to-understand sentences are:

1. Have something to say.

2. Know what you're talking about.

3. Say what you have to say as closely as possible to the way you speak.

At least at first. We speak in simple, easy-to-understand sentences. When we write like we speak, our messages are simple and easy to understand. But too many simple sentences in a row without the aid of eye contact, body gestures, and voice inflection can bore our readers. We risk sounding mechanical at best and childlike at worst.

Which brings us to the second characteristic of all good sentences:

Variety.

The purpose of variety is to avoid boring your readers with the monotony of similarly constructed sentences. If your writing consists only of a series of short declarative sentences, your readers will form the impression that you can think only in terms of simple statements, that you're incapable of seeing how things interrelate.

That having been said, it should also be noted that variety in and of itself is not a virtue; it only adds to the pleasure of reading a piece of writing that is already clear. In fact, if you pay careful attention to making your statements clear, variety will almost always result automatically.

But just to make sure your sentences are varied enough to maintain your readers' interest, here are some techniques you can use to avoid writing too many short sentences in a row:

- *Combine* two simple sentences into a longer one using a coordinating conjunction such as *and, or, but, for, so, yet,* and *nor.*

Instead of writing:

> William Carlos Williams was a poet. He was also a doctor who made house calls.

consider:

> William Carlos Williams was a poet, and he was also a doctor who made house calls.

However, when you use a coordinating conjunction to combine sentences, keep the following in mind:

– *Don't use a coordinating conjunction to connect two unrelated sentences.* It usually isn't effective and often confuses the reader.

> Consider:

> The supervisor started with the company in 1985, and he received a merit raise yesterday.

> What does this sentence tell the reader? Is the writer implying that the supervisor hasn't received a merit increase since 1985?

– *Choose the correct coordinating conjunction to link two thoughts.* Some coordinating conjunctions like *so* imply a cause-effect relationship. You wouldn't want to use *so* to imply a general relationship. *And* would be a better choice.

– *Don't link too many sentences into one sentence.* If you do, your sentence will ramble and your reader will lose track of the point you're trying to make.

- *Subordinate* one idea to another:

> Although William Carlos Williams was a poet, he was also a doctor who made house calls.

- *Embed* one idea within another:

> William Carlos Williams, a poet, was also a doctor who made house calls.

The best memos and letters contain a mixture of short, coordinated, subordinated, and embedded sentences. Any passage containing too many of one or the other will tire your readers or distract them from your message. So vary the length and construction of your sentences. Or consider one of these two rhetorical devices:

- *The question:*

  William Carlos Williams was a poet, but did you know he was also a doctor who made house calls?

- *The fragment:*

  William Carlos Williams was a doctor, but he was also something else. A poet.

  Although sentence fragments are considered grammatically incorrect, they can be used effectively when we write.

A third characteristic of a well-written sentence is:

Emphasis.

When you emphasize or stress certain ideas, you can add clarity to your writing by drawing your readers' attention to what is most important in your memo or letter. Appropriate emphasis is easy to achieve when you speak because of all the verbal and physical expressions you have to work with. When you write, however, you're limited to your choice of words, the way you arrange them, and a few graphic devices. To create emphasis in your sentences:

- *Save the best for last.* By putting your words, phrases, and clauses in ascending order of importance, you lead your readers toward a climax.

  Jan passed her exam, completed her thesis, and landed the first job she applied for.

- *Use parallel constructions.* Using grammatical constructions that are similar or complementary helps to emphasize your point.

    She was rewarded <u>not only</u> for her productivity <u>but also</u> for her customer service skills.

    We formed a committee <u>to</u> organize the workload, <u>to</u> develop a payment schedule, and <u>to</u> set a deadline for finishing the job.

    Weak attempts at parallelism not only produce grammatically incorrect sentences but also may confuse your reader.

    Incorrect:

    The trip was <u>relaxing</u> and <u>a joy</u>. (adjective and noun)

    Correct:

    The trip was <u>relaxing</u> and <u>enjoyable</u>. (two adjectives)

- *Interrupt the flow of the sentence.* By interrupting your thought with a word or phrase, you can emphasize a point or make your message more forceful.

    We need the payment—both this month's and last month's—by noon tomorrow.

- *Use simple graphics.* Italics, underlines, capital letters, and exclamation points all achieve emphasis. To use them too often in any single memo or letter, however, is to appear hysterical. And some devices actually detract from your message. Long passages written in all uppercase letters are difficult to read. Save them for short phrases or headings.

    The car is due at the airport. Now!

    You have one responsibility here: TO MAKE MONEY.

    Send us your date of birth by <u>August 4th</u>, and we'll process your application in time for your first class.

- *Begin every sentence strong.* Sometimes in trying to be thorough, we tend to back into our sentences, to introduce the most important point with a phrase or clause. Too many introductory phrases and clauses weaken the impact of the points you're trying to make. Instead of writing:

   If you do not include a self-addressed, stamped envelope, we will not be able to send you the information you requested.

consider:

   Send us a self-addressed, stamped envelope, and we'll send you the information you requested.

On the other hand, a strong introductory clause can increase emphasis when used effectively:

   If you don't pay your bill by the end of this month, we're turning your account over to a computer.

Similarly, so many of the same words begin so many sentences that the words have lost whatever power and energy they once may have had. Sentences, for example, beginning with *There is . . .* or *There are . . .* fall into this category. Instead of writing:

   There are three reasons for wanting to be a better editor: credibility, visibility, and image.

consider:

   Three reasons for wanting to be a better editor are credibility, visibility, and image.

Instead of writing:

   It appears as if John hasn't completed his report on time.

consider:

   John hasn't completed his report on time.

Emphasis, like variety, is effective only when it contributes to the whole memo or letter. Let your subject matter determine what should be emphasized. If you try to put emphasis in every sentence you write, you run the risk of undermining your credibility. Think, for example, of the boy who cried "Wolf!" so many times the villagers no longer believed him.

A Final Word About Sentences

Much is written about the low reading levels of our audiences. Nothing could be further from the truth. More people read today than ever before. And they are highly skilled. Newspapers, magazines, books, advertising, television, and movies all compete for our attention. Rarely do we read a sentence that wasn't crafted by a professional writer. The subjects may be dull, the treatments may be shallow, but the writing is almost always clear and direct. Clear and direct writing is what your readers have come to expect in effective memos and letters, and it's what you must strive to give them.

Try this exercise to determine the grade level your readers must have to understand your writing. Take anything you've written that has over 150 but not more than 200 words in it. Count the number of words with only one syllable, divide that number by 10, and subtract your answer from 20. If you come in at the number 12, you're writing at a twelfth-grade reading level. And what's the ideal reading level to make our memos and letters most effective? Sixth!

CLAUSES AND PHRASES

The Clause

A *clause* is a group of words containing a subject and a predicate. Some clauses form complete sentences. These clauses we call *independent*.

Clauses that do not form complete sentences are called *dependent*. Dependent clauses have something missing. They can't stand alone as sentences. They need more words to complete the thought they begin. Here are some examples of independent and dependent clauses:

Independent	*Dependent*
He can't get there.	If he can't get there
The mail is here.	Although the mail arrived
John hit the ball.	That John hit the ball
This is what she said.	Which is what she said

When these phrases are separated into columns, we have no trouble distinguishing the complete sentences (the independent clauses) from the incomplete sentences (the dependent clauses). The trouble occurs when we write quickly and, in our excitement for the subject or fear of an approaching deadline, we commit one of two kinds of errors. The first error we are likely to make is:

- *The run-on sentence.* The run-on sentence occurs when we join two complete sentences that should be separated by some kind of punctuation. These sentences are also called *fused sentences*. Here's what one looks like:

    Wally eats a pound of carrots every day his skin has turned orange.

Because there are two complete sentences here ("Wally eats a pound of carrots every day" and "His skin has turned orange"), they have to be written as two complete sentences. They must be separated by some kind of punctuation:

    A period: Wally eats a pound of carrots every day. His skin has turned orange.

    A semicolon: Wally eats a pound of carrots every day; his skin has turned orange.

A comma and a conjunction: Wally eats a pound of carrots every day, and his skin has turned orange.

Or these two separate sentences could be rewritten as one sentence:

Because he eats a pound of carrots every day, Wally's skin has turned orange.

What you can't do is leave the two separate sentences combined as if they were one complete thought.

The second error involving independent and dependent clauses that we are most likely to make is known as:

- *The sentence fragment.* A sentence fragment has a subject and a predicate, just as a complete sentence does, but the subject and predicate of the sentence fragment don't form a complete thought. Something is missing. For example:

  Although the letter arrived in time.

There should be more information here.

  Although the letter arrived in time, John did not read it.

  Although the letter arrived in time, Mary failed to submit her report by Tuesday.

Our problem with sentence fragments, however, is not that we can't detect incomplete thoughts. The problem is that we learned never to use sentence fragments. We speak in sentence fragments all the time and our listeners understand us. When we use similar sentence fragments in our writing, we make our messages even more powerful and effective. Even if they're grammatically incorrect!

"Even if they're grammatically incorrect!" is a sentence fragment, but you wouldn't want to turn this fragment into a complete sentence. To do so would weaken its impact. To determine whether to use a sentence fragment, you must know why you're using the fragment, and your reader must recognize why you're using the fragment.

The Phrase

A *phrase* is a group of words that form a thought. But because a phrase lacks a subject and a predicate, it can't stand alone as a sentence. There are many types of phrases, named according to the parts of speech they contain and how they function in a sentence. Examples of phrases are:

> on the desk (prepositional phrase)
>
> the large book (noun phrase)
>
> to own a house (infinitive phrase)
>
> building a company (gerund phrase)

Nevertheless, phrases—like sentence fragments—can sometimes be used as complete thoughts. For example:

> This company was going nowhere. Until now.
>
> To own a house. Once a dream, now a reality.

Even a word can be a sentence:

> When is it due? Yesterday.

Our major problem with phrases, however, is not whether to let them stand as complete thoughts. Our problem is we tend to jam too many of them into one sentence—especially in the opening sentences of memos and letters.

Because we've been told that good opening sentences should give the reader a complete idea of what any memo or letter is about, we often find ourselves trying to squeeze more information into these sentences than our readers can easily absorb. The most common way of adding too much information to a sentence is through the *prepositional phrase.*

A *prepositional phrase* consists of a connective word (*in, on, of, to, with*) linked to a noun or an adjective and a noun. Examples of prepositional phrases are:

in the book

on the table

of the company

to the meeting

with the money

for the children

over the fence

under the chair

A sentence containing too many prepositional phrases in a row tires the reader. Consider this sentence that appeared recently in a newspaper:

John Craft, an administrator for 20 years with the School Planning Council of Hampshire County in western Massachusetts, said he will begin work on a project of AIDS awareness in the county's school system for the next academic year if the current fiscal budget remains intact.

Unless you're "of the people, by the people, and for the people," Abraham Lincoln, limit your prepositional phrases to no more than two or three in a row.

Clauses and phrases may also be *restrictive* or *nonrestrictive*.

A *restrictive* clause or phrase is one that provides information that is essential to a sentence's meaning. If you were to take out the clause, the meaning of the sentence would change.

The bill that came in today's mail is due by October 20.

That came in today's mail identifies a particular bill—not one that came yesterday, not one that came last week, but the one that came today. Notice that commas are not necessary for setting off essential clauses.

A *nonrestrictive* clause or phrase contains information that is not essential to the meaning of the sentence. Commas separate nonrestrictive clauses from the rest of the sentence.

The bill, <u>which she paid yesterday,</u> was for repairs on Mike's computer.

In this sentence, *which she paid yesterday* does not contain information that is essential for explaining what the bill was for.

Word Usage

In the beginning was the word. And there's been a lot of confusion since. Why, for example, *no one* should be written as two words and *nobody* as one has little to do with reason. It has to do with usage.

And our usage of words changes constantly. So does the standard acceptance of words. One writer's slang can be another writer's powerful expression. If a word is likely to offend even a few readers, however, it is probably best to avoid it.

COMMONLY CONFUSED WORDS

Here are some commonly confused words and what you need to know to keep them clear in your mind as well as your readers'.

A, An. *A* is used before words beginning with a consonant sound.

> <u>a</u> car, <u>a</u> euphemism, <u>a</u> poem

An is used before words beginning with a vowel sound.

> <u>an</u> hour, <u>an</u> arrow

A lot, Alot. *A lot*, when you mean "many," is two words. *Alot* as one word is the name of a particular kind of camel. Avoid the second when you mean the first.

Actually. Avoid using *actually* as an intensifier.

> He <u>actually</u> could use a raise.

Actually expresses a contrast between what is fact and what is opinion.

> He says he wants a raise, but <u>actually</u> he doesn't deserve one.

Ad. A shortened form for *advertisement*, *ad* came into popular speech through journalism headlines. The same is true for *auto*, *exam*, *gym*, *quote*, *phone*, and *Xmas*. In writing, consider using the longer forms of these words.

Adapt, Adopt. *Adapt* means "to adjust."

> She <u>adapted</u> quickly to the new job.

Adopt means "to borrow or to put into practice."

> She <u>adopted</u> his methods.

An exception is when you "adopt" children. They can't be borrowed or put into practice.

Adverse, Averse. Something that is *adverse* is something that is "unfavorable."

> Those were <u>adverse</u> conditions.

To be *averse* to something is to "have a dislike or distaste" for it.

> He is <u>averse</u> to cutting taxes.

The noun form of averse is used more commonly, however.

> He has an <u>aversion</u> for low taxes.

4

Advice, Advise. *Advice* is a noun meaning "suggestions" or "recommendations."

> That was good <u>advice</u>.

Advise is a verb meaning "to suggest" or "to recommend."

> Will she <u>advise</u> you?

Affect, Effect. *Affect* is used only as a verb, meaning "to influence" or "to assume."

> That deeply <u>affected</u> him.

> He <u>affected</u> a Southern accent.

Effect can be used as either a verb meaning "to cause" or a noun meaning "a result."

> He <u>effected</u> the change.

> The change had an exhilarating <u>effect</u> on him.

Aggravate. In popular speech, *aggravate* is sometimes used to mean "to annoy."

> You <u>aggravate</u> me.

In writing, we should stick to the traditional "to intensify" or "to make worse."

> That <u>aggravated</u> the situation.

All, All of. It's not necessary to use *of* after *all* unless the word that follows is a pronoun.

> <u>All of</u> them (pronoun) blinked at the same time.

> <u>All</u> the group members blinked at the same time.

All right, Alright. *Alright* used to be "alwrong." Now, because so many people misspell the word, both spellings are listed in the dictionary. Nevertheless, *all right* is still considered the standard in business and industry.

Allusion, Illusion. An *allusion* is a "reference" to something.

Her <u>allusion</u> to your book was effective.

An *illusion* is a "false impression."

The bank created the <u>illusion</u> that it was solvent.

Among, Between. *Among* is used when referring to more than two.

We had many options to choose <u>among</u>.

Between is used when comparing, choosing, or referring in other ways to groups of two people, places, or things.

We had to choose <u>between</u> an IRA and a Keogh account.

Amount, Number. *Amount* refers to things in bulk.

A small <u>amount</u> of sand will fill the pail.

Number refers to individual items that can be counted.

A large <u>number</u> of children will attend the recital.

Anxious, Eager. *Anxious* implies "worry, fear, or concern."

She was <u>anxious</u> to receive her annual review.

Eager means "enthusiastic desire or interest."

She was <u>eager</u> to go to the amusement park.

Assure, Ensure, Insure. All mean "to make certain" or "to guarantee," but *assure* is used where people are concerned.

I <u>assure</u> you that everything is all right.

Ensure and *insure* are used when the focus is on financial matters.

He failed to <u>insure</u> his house against fire.

Recently, however, *insure* has appeared almost exclusively with matters of insurance, while *ensure* has been applied to other matters.

You need to buy a thermometer to <u>ensure</u> that your car will not overheat.

4

Bad, Badly. *Bad* is an adjective.

It was a <u>bad</u> proposal.

Badly is an adverb.

He writes <u>badly</u>.

Bad is the correct form after verbs of sensation (I *feel*, You *look*, He *smells*, She *sounds*, It *tastes*). To say "The meat smells *bad*" is to say that the meat has an odor. To say "The meat smells *badly*" is to imply that the meat has a nose.

Because, That. After words such as *reason, excuse,* and *explanation,* the correct choice is *that.*

The reason Judy quit is <u>that</u> she hated him.

Can, May. *Can* indicates "ability to do."

I <u>can</u> go to the store.

May expresses "permission to do."

<u>May</u> I go to the store?

Capital, Capitol. *Capital* means "invested money."

She lacked the <u>capital</u> to open her own business.

Capital also means "chief in importance," as in "a *capital* offense." But *capital* also refers to "the city in which a central government is located."

Boston is the <u>capital</u> of Massachusetts.

However, the specific building that houses the central government is called the *capitol.*

The Massachusetts legislature approved the funds necessary to restore the <u>capitol</u> dome.

Cite, Sight, Site. To *cite* is "to quote."

He proved his point by <u>citing</u> several authorities.

Sight refers to "vision."

The building is no longer in <u>sight</u>.

A *site* is a "location."

Bring the tools to that <u>site</u>.

Common, Mutual. *Common* refers to "what we share with others" (*common* sense); *mutual* means "reciprocal" (*mutual* trust).

Compliment, Complement. A *compliment* is a "statement of praise."

That was quite a <u>compliment</u> you received.

A *complement* is "something that completes or supplements something else."

They <u>complement</u> each other.

One way to keep the difference between these two words straight is to remember that the word spelled with "i" refers to the things "I" like to hear about myself.

Continual, Continuous. *Continual* means "frequently repeated action with pauses, interruptions, or intermissions."

The photocopier <u>continually</u> breaks down.

Continuous means "frequently repeated action without pauses, interruptions, or intermissions."

The stream moves <u>continuously</u> past our door.

Council, Counsel. A *council* is a "governing body of people."

The <u>council</u> meets on Thursday.

To *counsel* is "to advise."

She <u>counseled</u> him in ways to avoid getting laid off.

4

Course, Coarse. *Course* is a "path or direction" or "something one studies."

    I am taking a <u>course</u> in biology next semester.

Coarse means "composed of large particles" or "rough."

    The sandpaper is <u>coarse</u>.

Criteria, Criterion. *Criteria* is the plural of *criterion* and should be used with a plural verb.

    The <u>criteria</u> are met.

Data, Datum. *Data* is the plural of *datum* and should be used with a plural verb, although it is becoming increasingly popular to use *data* as a collective noun requiring a singular verb.

    The <u>data</u> are collected.

    The <u>data</u> is complete.

Different from, Different than. Used interchangeably for the past 300 years.

Disinterested, Uninterested. *Disinterested* means "unbiased" or "impartial."

    Every member of the jury was supposed to be <u>disinterested</u>.

Uninterested means "lacking interest."

    He was <u>uninterested</u> in the subject.

Eminent, Imminent. *Eminent* means "prestigious."

    She is an <u>eminent</u> scientist.

Imminent means "near."

    The hurricane is <u>imminent</u>.

Ex, Former. *Ex* is used with the title of the person who held a position immediately before the person who currently holds it. *Former* designates an earlier titleholder. To say that "Abraham Lincoln is a *former* U.S. president" is correct because Lincoln did not hold the position immediately before our current president.

Farther, Further. Interchangeable in practice, *farther* used to be reserved for physical distances and *further* for degrees.

> The hotel is <u>farther</u> than the gas station. (physical distance)

> One <u>further</u> note (degree)

Further can also mean "to promote," and only *further* is correct when meaning "in addition."

> And, <u>further</u>, the bill is not correct.

Fewer, Less. *Fewer* measures numbers.

> There are <u>fewer</u> people here now.

Less measures quantity.

> There was <u>less</u> milk in the container today.

To say, as many writers do, "There are *less* people here today than yesterday" is to announce that the people who showed up today are missing parts of their bodies.

First, Firstly. When enumerating ideas, don't add *ly* to *first*, *second*, *third*, etc.

Good, Well. *Good* is an adjective.

> He received a <u>good</u> recommendation from the committee.

Well is both an adjective and an adverb. It is considered an adjective when used to refer to a person's state of health.

> She did as <u>well</u> as she could on the exam.

> The child did not feel <u>well</u>.

4

Healthy, Healthful. Both are adjectives, but *healthy* refers to people or animals that are "in good health."

>The children were <u>healthy</u>.

Healthful refers to a climate, food, or lifestyle that is "beneficial to health."

>Carrots are a <u>healthful</u> food.

Have you ever heard of a carrot that was *healthy*? If so, the carrot was enjoying good health!

Hopefully. *Hopefully* is always acceptable when meaning "in a hopeful manner."

>Marge asked <u>hopefully</u> for a raise.

However, the word is a topic of controversy when used at the beginning of a sentence to mean the popular "I hope."

><u>Hopefully</u>, I'll get to the airport in time.

Some writers claim that using *hopefully* in this way is no different than using *obviously, certainly, actually,* or other words that modify a whole sentence. Avoid using *hopefully* in this way if you'd rather avoid conflict.

If, Whether. *If* is often used in speech to mean *whether.* Use *whether* when you write.

>I don't know <u>whether</u> I should go to the bank yet.

Imply, Infer. *Imply* means "to suggest without stating directly."

>His smile <u>implied</u> a friendly attitude.

Infer means "to reach a conclusion."

>I <u>inferred</u> from his smile that he was friendly.

In regard to, As regards. Both are acceptable, but many writers today choose the simpler *regarding.*

>The personnel director sent out a memo <u>regarding</u> the new insurance plan.

Irregardless. Considered redundant for *regardless*. Avoid. This doesn't mean, however, that all words beginning with *ir* are redundant. Consider these words, for example:

irrational	unreasonable
irreconcilable	incapable of being won over
irredeemable	cannot be reclaimed
irreducible	cannot be made smaller
irrefutable	cannot be refuted
irregular	asymmetrical
irrelevant	not applicable
irremediable	cannot be corrected
irremissible	cannot be pardoned
irreparable	cannot be repaired
irreplaceable	cannot be substituted for
irrepressible	cannot be controlled
irreproachable	having no faults
irresistible	too powerful to be resisted
irresolute	hesitant, undecided
irrespective	without regard to
irresponsible	having no sense of responsibility
irreverent	lacking respect for
irrevocable	cannot be altered or revoked
irrigate	to artificially water crops or to wash out with water
irritate	to annoy

4

Its, It's. *Its* is a possessive pronoun.

The company makes <u>its</u> daily bank deposit at 10 a.m.

It's is a contraction meaning "it is."

<u>It's</u> snowing outside today.

Later, Latter. *Later* has to do with time.

I'll see you <u>later</u>.

Latter means "the second of two people, places, or things."

The <u>latter</u> proposal was chosen.

Lay, Lie. To *lay* is "to put."

<u>Lay</u> that on my desk.

To *lie* is "to rest" or "to say something that isn't true."

<u>Lie</u> down.

Don't <u>lie</u>.

Lay (to put)	*Lie* (to rest)
lay	lie
laid	lay
laid	lain
laying	lying

Like, As. Writers who wish to play it safe still use *like* as a preposition and *as* as a conjunction. The colloquial "He looked *like* he might be a pro" may still raise a few eyebrows.

He looked <u>like</u> a pro.

He looked <u>as</u> if he might be a pro.

Maybe, May be. *Maybe* means "perhaps."

<u>Maybe</u> I'll see you.

May be is a verb having to do with possibility.

Whether I see you <u>may be</u> determined by others.

Media, Medium. *Media* is the plural form of *medium*.

Myself. Use only when the subject of the sentence is also the receiver of the action.

> I hurt <u>myself</u>.

Avoid the popular:

> He invited Dave and <u>myself</u>.

Of, Have. Don't use *of* instead of *have* with verbs. Write would *have*, should *have*, could *have*, not would *of*, should *of*, could *of*.

Per. Outdated business jargon. Avoid.

Person, People. When you're referring to more than one person, *people* usually sounds more friendly than *persons*. And always use *people* when referring to a large group.

Practical, Practicable. Interchangeable in meaning, *practical* is the favorite in usage.

Principal, Principle. *Principal*, meaning "chief" or "main," refers to the head of a school or to money used as capital. *Principle* means "rule" or "law" or "doctrine." To remember the difference: "The *principal* is my *pal* and so is money."

Raise, Rise. To *raise* something is to "push or lift it up."

> He <u>raised</u> the roof with his shouting.

To *rise* is "to get up" or "move upward."

> <u>Rise</u> and shine.

Respectfully, Respectively. *Respectfully* means "with respect."

> I <u>respectfully</u> submit . . .

Respectively means "in the sequence mentioned previously."

> The proposals were submitted on May 15th, May 22nd, and June 1st; consider them <u>respectively</u>.

4

Set, Sit. *Set* means "to place something somewhere"; *sit* means "to be seated" or "to be in a resting position."

Set (to place)	*Sit* (to be seated)
set	sit
set	sat
set	sat
setting	sitting

Shall, Will. Interchangeable in meaning, *shall* used to appear with the personal pronouns *I* and *we*, while *will* was used with *you, he, she, it,* and *they.* Perhaps because it is rarely used today, *shall* carries more force than *will.*

Stationary, Stationery. Something that is *stationary* is "fixed in one place."

The wall unit is <u>stationary</u>.

Stationery is letter paper.

We need more <u>stationery</u> before the letters can be sent out.

Than, Then. Use *than* when making comparisons. Use *then* to mean "therefore," "as a result," or "a point in time" or to indicate sequence.

Jerry is smarter <u>than</u> Mark.

Type the letter; <u>then</u> mail it.

That, Which. Both words are pronouns that refer to inanimate objects, places, or animals. *That* introduces restrictive clauses; *which* introduces nonrestrictive clauses. However, *which* is being used more and more to introduce restrictive clauses as well.

The cup <u>that</u> is on my desk is clean.

That cup, <u>which</u> was a gift from my colleagues, is clean.

The, A. Use *the* to denote something specific.

Bring me <u>the</u> pen from my desk.

Use *a* to denote something general.

> Bring me <u>a</u> pen from my desk.

In the first example, there is only one pen on the desk; in the second, any one of a number of pens will do.

Their, There, They're. *Their* shows possession.

> <u>Their</u> bus has arrived.

There means "at that place or point."

> We're going over <u>there</u>.

They're is a contraction for *they are.*

> <u>They're</u> more eager than we expected.

Toward, Towards. Interchangeable, though *toward* is the choice of tradition.

Unique. *Unique* means "one of a kind, having no equal," but in popular speech it can mean "unusual," "remarkable," "rare," or "extraordinary." If you mean "unusual," "remarkable," "rare," or "extraordinary," say so.

Utilize, Utilization. Awkward ways of saying *use.*

Who, Whom. See discussion in Chapter 7 on syntax.

Who's, Whose. *Who*'s is a contraction for *who is* or *who has.*

> <u>Who's</u> that?

Whose is the possessive form of who.

> <u>Whose</u> glove is this?

Your, you're. *Your* is the possessive case of you.

> Is that *your* book?

You're is a contraction for *you are.*

> <u>You're</u> planning on being there, aren't you?

4

BIG WORDS VS. SMALL WORDS

Don't use a big word when a small word will do. You run the risk of sounding pompous or artificial. To test the effect a word might have on your readers, take the word out of the context in which it usually appears and give it the same meaning in another context. Imagine, for example, rushing home to "interface" with your kids. If it looks bad on the page and sounds bad to your ear, it may look and sound worse to your reader. Here are some commonly used big words and some corresponding substitutes you may wish to consider:

accumulate (gather)

acquaint (tell)

activate (start)

additional (more)

adhere to (follow)

aggregate (total)

amalgamate (merge)

ameliorate (improve)

anticipate (expect)

ascertain (learn)

cognizant (know)

commence (begin)

concur (agree)

configuration (shape)

conjecture (guess)

equivalent (equal)

expeditious (fast)

factor (fact)

feasible (likely)

initial (first)

interface (relate)

locate (find)

magnitude (size)

manifest (show)

materialize (occur, happen)

modification (change)

necessitate (require)

optimum (best)

personnel (people)

peruse (study)

presently (now)

prior to (before)

subsequent (later)

substantiate (prove)

sufficient (adequate)

terminate (end)

transpire (happen)

utilize (use)

REDUNDANT EXPRESSIONS

Don't be redundant. Words are like inflated money: the more you use, the less they're worth. Eliminate words that repeat your message:

absolutely essential (essential)

actual experience (experience)

actual fact (fact)

advance planning (planning)

assembled together (assembled)

basic essentials (basics or essentials)

brief in duration (brief)

completely opposite (opposite)

consensus of opinion (consensus)

continue to remain (remain)

end result (result)

few in number (few)

final conclusion (conclusion)

first began (began)

mutual cooperation (cooperation)

necessary essentials (essentials)

other alternative (alternative)

past experience (experience)

personal opinion (opinion)

plan ahead (plan)

point in time (now/then)

refer back (refer)

surplus left over (surplus)

true facts (facts or truth)

4

CLICHÉD EXPRESSIONS

Don't use clichéd expressions. These expressions were effective when they were first created. That's why they became popular. That's also why they've become stale and no longer have the power they once possessed. Avoid or find new expressions for the ones that repetition has sapped of energy:

acknowledge the receipt of

at your earliest convenience

benefit of the doubt

by the same token

circumstances beyond control

do not hesitate to call

enclosed please find

few and far between

foregone conclusion

gratefully acknowledge

hastily summoned

inextricably linked

in no uncertain terms

in reference to

It has come to our attention . . .

keeping your options open

pales by comparison

please be advised that

pros and cons

pursuant to our conversation

regrettable incident

remedy the situation

sweeping changes

trials and tribulations

unprecedented situation

viable alternative

WORDY EXPRESSIONS

Don't be wordy. Wordy phrases work to our advantage when we speak—they give us time to think of what we want to say next. But in writing, they slow our readers down and make them wonder why we're not getting to the point of our message. Here are some common wordy phrases and the corresponding substitutes you may wish to consider using:

a great number of (many)

a majority of (most)

a sufficient number (enough)

as a matter of fact (in fact)

as of this date (by)

at a later date (later)

at the present time (now)

at your earliest convenience (give specific date)

attached please find (attached is)

by the time that (when)

called attention to the fact (reminded)

due to the fact that (because)

during the month of May (May)

exactly alike (identical)

except in a small number of cases (few)

for the purpose of (to)

for the reason that (because)

give consideration to (consider)

I am in receipt of (I received)

in a position to (able)

in addition to (also/besides)

4

in a timely manner (soon)

in conjunction with (with)

in order to (to)

in the amount of (check for)

in the course of (during)

in the event that (if, when, should)

in the majority of cases (most)

in view of the fact that (considering)

inasmuch as (because, since, as)

is in excess of (exceeds)

is negligent in (neglect)

it has been brought to my attention (I learned)

it is clear that (clearly)

it is incumbent on me to (I must)

it would appear that (it seems)

it would not be unreasonable to assume (I assume)

make a determination (determine)

make a purchase (buy)

make contact with (meet)

make provision for (provide)

of minor importance (unimportant)

offer a solution to (propose)

offer a suggestion (suggest)

on behalf of (meet)

on two different occasions (twice)

per your request (you asked)

pertaining to (about)

pursuant to (following)

provide compensation for (pay)

since the time when (since)

subsequent to (after, following)

take appropriate measures (act)

take under consideration (consider)

thanking you in advance (thank you)

the only difference being (except)

through the use of (by)

until such time as (until)

we wish to thank you for (thank you)

with reference to (about)

with regard to (about)

within the realm of possibility (possible/possibly)

One way to measure how wordy we can be is to consider some of the many ways we've created just to say *because*:

based on the fact that

due to the fact that

for the reason that

in consideration of the fact that

in light of the fact that

inasmuch as

on account of

owing to the fact that

4

VAGUE EXPRESSIONS

Don't use vague expressions. Many words don't communicate a *clear* message because they are vague. Tell your readers *specifically* what you mean. Consider how the expressions on the right communicate a much clearer message than those on the left.

as soon as possible (by 5 o'clock)

frequently used (used six times a day)

highly recommended (My pediatrician recommends it.)

I'll call you soon. (I'll call you by noon tomorrow.)

quick service (24-hour turnaround)

satisfied client (The client referred us to three of his friends.)

substantial savings (saved $100 off retail)

very good response (We received a 10 percent greater response than we projected.)

SEXIST LANGUAGE

Don't be sexist. Do you still refer to men as "men" but women as "girls"? Do you distinguish between "lawyers" and "lady lawyers"? Do you call women by their first names and men by their last even though they may hold similar positions in a company? Do you think the fuss over sexist writing is trivial? If you answered "yes" to any of these questions, you need to catch up with the times. Sexist language patronizes, implies second-class status, and is demeaning. Here's one suggestion to help you on your way:

Avoid gender references.

If you have to refer to gender, however, consider these tips:

Use parallel language.

Instead of:	Write:
men and ladies	men and women
man and wife	husband and wife
John Dow and Mary	John Dow and Mary Ward

Use terms that include both sexes.

Instead of:	Write:
mankind	people
manpower	personnel
mothering	nurturing
average man	average person
chairman	chair, chairperson
foreman	supervisor
salesman	sales representative
policeman	police officer
mailman	letter carrier
fireman	firefighter
newsman	journalist
to man	to operate

4

Don't use a feminine pronoun with a neuter noun.

Neuter nouns now take neuter pronouns. Avoid sentences such as:

> The old car did her best, but the hill was too much for her.

> She's a proud country that's fallen on hard times.

> I got her (the boat) into the bay well before the storm hit.

Cars, boats, ships, countries, waterways, and the like no longer take feminine pronouns.

Use nonsexist salutations.

There is no substitute for using a person's name when you address your letters. Use a person's name and spell that person's name correctly, and you have that person on your side before he or she reads the first word of your letter.

When you don't know your reader's gender, however, you may wish to consider these alternatives:

- *Inclusive titles*. The standard salutation in a business letter is "Dear Sir or Madam." "To whom it may concern:" is now considered dated. Nevertheless, you may wish to use one of these other inclusive salutations:

> Dear Personnel Manager:

> Dear Customer Service Representative:

> Dear Seminar Participant:

> Dear Homeowner:

> Dear Colleague:

> Dear Client:

- *Generic greetings*. Many writers, uncomfortable with calling someone they don't know "Dear," are opening their letters with:

> Good Morning!

> Greetings!

- *Subject lines.* Still another popular alternative is to replace the salutation with a subject line:

    RE: Your Individual Retirement Account

    RE: Your National Public Radio Pledge

    RE: Government Funding for AIDS

- *Skipping the salutation.* Some writers eliminate the salutation and subject line. They go right into the message. These same writers often leave out the complimentary closing as well on the grounds that no one reads it.

The problem with "Dear Sir or Madam:" inclusive titles, generic greetings, subject lines, and diving right into the message is that many people see these strategies as impersonal. No matter how inventive they may be, they cannot equal the effect of using a person's name.

Nothing can.

But when you do know the name of the person you're writing to, which form of address do you use?

- *Ms. or Mrs.?* The standard form of address is "Ms." If your reader wishes to be addressed as "Mrs.," she will include "(Mrs.)" in the name printed beneath her signature:

    Sincerely,

    (Mrs.) Barbara Peterson

- *Mr. or Ms.* If you can't find out whether the "Pat" or "Chris" you're addressing is a man or a woman, consider:

    Dear Pat Jones

    Dear Chris Thompson

    Dear M. J. Smith

Avoid too many "his or her" constructions.

The most common problem with sexist statements is demonstrated in the following sentence construction:

Each supervisor must hand in his proposal.

Because we've been taught to choose the masculine case when pronouns include both men and women, the traditionally correct choice in this sentence construction is *his*. But *his* offends the sensibilities of people living in our age of enlightened consciousness. To substitute the word *they* is now considered grammatically correct, according to no less an august publication than the *Oxford English Dictionary*, but we would risk offending many traditional grammarians if we used *they*. A "supervisor" isn't a *they*. To satisfy both the enlightened and the traditional, consider these alternatives:

- Use the word *or*.

  Each supervisor must hand in his <u>or</u> her proposal.

- Use the plural form.

  All supervisors must hand in <u>their</u> proposals.

- Use the words *the*, *a*, or *an*.

  Each supervisor must hand in <u>a</u> proposal.

- Use the words *you* or *your*.

  As a supervisor, you must hand in <u>your</u> proposal.

A Final Word on Sexist Language

If you still think it's appropriate to use the masculine pronoun when referring to both men and women, consider this statement:

Modern man has all he can do to get up in the morning, wash, put on his make-up, make breakfast for his family, and get everybody off to school and work early so he'll keep his appointment with his gynecologist.

BIASED LANGUAGE

Don't use words that show a bias toward races, creeds, people of certain ages, and those who are handicapped or disabled. Because so many of the words that reveal these biases are slang and signs of hateful ignorance, we already avoid most of them. There are some words, however, that can cause offense without our being aware of it. The word *Oriental*, for example, offends many Asians because of its traditional association with the unknown and mysterious. Use *Asians*. Similarly, *African-American* is currently the preferred choice of many people who used to be called *Afro-American*, *colored*, and *black*.

Some people use the words *handicapped* and *disabled* interchangeably. But there is a difference. A person who is disabled is physically or emotionally impaired. Someone who can overcome his or her disability is no longer *disabled*. He or she is now handicapped. Although *disabled* and *handicapped* are a big improvement over *crippled*, *deaf*, *dumb*, and *retarded*, they still carry negative connotations and offend some people. Many of these people prefer *special needs* or *physically challenged*.

Special needs and *physically challenged* haven't gained the same acceptance as *Asian* or *African-American*, however, because they have caused confusion in some of the contexts in which they are used. The Philadelphia Board of Education, for example, replaced its "Office for Disabled Persons" with "Office for People with Special Needs" and found itself flooded with homeless people. The board then changed the name to the "Office for the Physically Challenged" only to be swamped with teachers who felt threatened by their students. Now the sign says "Office for Disabled Persons."

4

POSITIVE WORDS CONVEY A POSITIVE MESSAGE

Use positive words rather than negative words. Words such as *misinformed* and *questionable* make our readers want to distance themselves from our messages. Words such as *admirable* and *agreeable* draw our readers into our messages.

Instead of telling your readers what you can't do, tell them what you can do. "Send us your completed application form by the 15th of this month, and you'll hear from us within two weeks after we receive it" is more effective than "If you don't send us your completed application by the 15th of this month, we won't be able to process it until February."

Note: The second sentence can be more effective if your reader hasn't responded to your positively worded statement. The difference is tone.

Tone determines how our readers think and feel about us. It is the image we project. Nietzsche once said that we very rarely object to the words of any message but rather to the tone in which the message is delivered. Here is a list of negative- and positive-sounding words:

Negative Words

No	Fault	Should	Allege
Not	Inadequate	Claim	Complain
Never	Inferior	My lawyer	Error
Couldn't	Insist	Wrong	Neglect
Wouldn't	Demand	Overlook	Oversight
Shouldn't	Lie	Must	Fail
Can't	Misinform	Failure	Jargon
Don't	Mistake	Won't	Gobbledygook

Business Writing Clichés

Positive Words			
Yes	Gladly	Comfort	Thank you
Admire	Happy	Good	Value
Respect	Grateful	Great	Welcome
Deserve	Gratitude	Please	At no charge
Agree	Pleasure	Kind	Congratulations
Benefit	Satisfy	Clear Words	Personal Words

A FINAL WORD ON WORDS

Care about them. They're your tools for making a good impression in every memo and letter that you write. Use them well, and they will serve you well.

CHAPTER 5

Spelling

F ew things undermine our credibility as much as misspelled words. Ironically, we're not that bad at spelling. More often than not, we make typographical errors and don't notice them when we proofread our memos and letters.

The reason we miss the typographical errors is that we put those words on the page; we know the direction they're taking us. Because we know the context in which the words appear, our eyes have a tendency to see just the first few letters of the words. Then, when the word has registered in our minds, we skip to the first few letters of the next word. Sometimes, even though our eyes may be scanning all the words, our minds are focusing on only the initial letters of whole groups of words. This is why most spelling mistakes occur in the middle or at the end of words. It's not that we don't know how to spell these words; we just aren't good at catching the typographical errors. To identify our typographical errors, we have to take each word out of the context in which it appears. The section on proofreading in Chapter 1 offers several effective methods for catching your typographical errors.

Now that you know how to catch your spelling mistakes, here are a few spelling rules to help you correct them. Don't try to learn these rules; the exceptions alone will drive you crazy. Instead, keep them handy for use as a reference.

I BEFORE E EXCEPT AFTER C

Except in words that sound like *hay*. Examples of these words are *neighbor* and *weigh*.

SEDE, CEED, AND CEDE

Supersede is the only word ending in *sede*.

Exceed, proceed, and *succeed* are the only words ending in *ceed*.

All the other words ending with this sound end in *cede*.

ADDING PREFIXES TO A WORD

When adding a prefix to a word, neither the spelling of the prefix nor the spelling of the word changes.

mis + spell = misspell

un + necessary = unnecessary

ADDING SUFFIXES TO A WORD

- When adding a suffix to a word ending in *y* preceded by a consonant, change the *y* to *i* before adding the suffix.

    deny   denies

    study   studies

Unless the suffix begins with *i*. Then you keep the *y*.

deny	denying
study	studying
hobby	hobbyist

- When adding a suffix to a word ending in *e*, drop the *e* before suffixes beginning with a vowel.

wage	waging
combine	combination

If the suffix begins with a consonant, keep the *e*.

entire	entirely
manage	management

Exceptions to this rule include:

manageable, changeable

argument, judgment, truly

acknowledgment

- When adding a suffix to a word that is only one syllable long or a word that is accented on the last syllable, double the final consonant of the word before adding the suffix.

shop	shopped
stop	stopped
begin	beginning
occur	occurred

FORMING THE PLURALS OF WORDS

- For most words, just add *s*.

book	books
pen	pens

- For words ending in *s*, *sh*, *ss*, *ch*, *z*, or *x*, add *es*.

boss	bosses
church	churches
bus	buses
dish	dishes
buzz	buzzes
box	boxes

- For words ending in *o* preceded by a consonant, add *es*.

veto	vetoes
tomato	tomatoes

  Note: There are so many exceptions to this rule that you should consult a dictionary if you have any doubt.

- For words ending in *y*:

  If the letter in front of the *y* is a vowel, just add *s*.

attorney	attorneys

  If the letter in front of the *y* is a consonant, change the *y* to *i* and add *es*.

ally	allies

5

- To form the plural of compound terms, add the *s* or *es* to the most important word:

attorney at law	attorneys at law
grant in aid	grants in aid
assistant attorney	assistant attorneys
trade union	trade unions

- To form the plurals of abbreviations, titles, figures, and symbols, add either an *s* or an *'s*. Let what looks best on the page and what will cause the least confusion for your reader determine your choice. Consider avoiding *'s* whenever possible, however, as it might be mistaken for showing possession.

The three Rs	or	The three R's
Three SOSs	or	Three SOS's
All OKs	or	All OK's
Two CODs	or	Two COD's

In the first and last examples, both choices seem acceptable; in the middle examples, the second choice seems to make the most sense.

BRITISH VS. AMERICAN SPELLING

In the United States, the American way is correct; in Great Britain, the British spelling takes prominence. If you are writing to people in Great Britain, Canada, New Zealand, Australia, or a former British colony where English is the standard language (India, Zimbabwe, Jamaica, the Caymans, the Bahamas, etc.), as a courtesy you may wish to consider using a British dictionary. Or you might consider keeping a reference list of words that you've noticed through your correspondence are spelled differently.

British Spelling	American Spelling
counselling	counseling
travelling	traveling
judgement	judgment
labour	labor
harbour	harbor

A FINAL WORD ON SPELLING

Write only the words you would say. Very rarely do we say a word we don't also know how to spell. Compare the degree of spelling difficulty between the words we tend to use when we write with those we use when we speak:

When we write:	When we speak:
activate	start
additional	more
apprise	tell
curtail	slow
fabricate	make
initiate	begin
manifest	show
necessitate	compel
perspective	view
proceed	go
ramification	result
request	ask
terminate	end
utilize	use

The more letters there are in any word, the more chances there are for a spelling mistake to creep in.

Consider using these tips to help you improve your spelling of words that give you difficulty:

- Find out what it is about the word that gives you trouble and then develop a gimmick for remembering the correct spelling. If you can't remember whether *judgment* is spelled with or without an *e*, remember *eliminate* and you'll know not to use the *e*.

- Keep a list of your most commonly misspelled words and refer to it often.

- If you know you often misspell names or words that are common to your business, add them to your computer's spell checker.

Remember, the bottom-line rule for spelling is:

When in doubt, look it up!

Spelling

a lot
absence
accommodate
accompanying
achievement
acquaintance
acquire
across
adolescent
advantageous
advertise
affect
aggravate
aisle
all right
analysis
analyze
annually
answer
apparently
appreciable
approximate
arbitrary
architect

argument
athletic
attorney
autumn
auxiliary
bankruptcy
basically
beginning
believe
beneficiary
benefited
bureaucracy
calendar
campaign
canceled
catalog
category
cemetery
changeable
chronological
coincidence
collateral
colonel
column

commitment
committee
concede
conscience
conscientious
conscious
consensus
continuous
criticism
criticized
debt
debtor
defendant
deficit
definite
definitely
descendant
describe
detrimental
develop
development
dilemma
disappoint
dissatisfied

dissimilar
ecstasy
effect
eighth
eligible
embarrass
embarrassed
emphasize
empty
enumerate
environment
exaggerate
excellent
exhaustible
exhibition
existence
exorbitant
experience
extraordinary
facsimile
familiar
fascinating
February
foreign

5

Commonly Misspelled Words

foresee
forfeit
forty
fourteen
fourth
fulfill
government
grammar
grievous
guarantee
guardian
harass
hemorrhage
hors d'oeuvre
hygiene
hypocrisy
immediately
innocuous
inoculate
interest
interruption
invariably
irrelevant
itinerary

judgment
knowledgeable
labeled
laboratory
leisure
leisurely
liable
liaison
library
license
lieutenant
likable
maintenance
maneuver
mileage
miniature
miscellaneous
mischievous
misspell
mortgage
necessary
negotiate
neither
ninety

ninth
noticeable
occasion
occasionally
occurrence
occurring
omelet
omission
opinion
oppressed
pamphlet
panicky
parallel
partially
pastime
permissible
perseverance
persuade
phenomenal
physician
picnicking
plausible
possessions
possibly

precede
precedent
prerogative
pretense
privilege
procedure
proceed
programmed
pronunciation
psychiatric
psychological
publicly
quantity
questionnaire
receipt
receive
received
recipient
recommend
reference
relevant
renowned
rescind
restaurant

Spelling

résumé	strictly	theater
rhythm	subpoena	thoroughly
schedule	subtlety	through
secretary	subtly	totaled
separate	succeed	tragedy
sergeant	success	transferred
siege	supersede	truly
similar	surgeon	unmanageable
simultaneous	surprise	used to
skillful	surveillance	Wednesday
souvenir	susceptible	wholly
sponsor	technique	wield
strength	temperature	yield

Punctuation

Prior to the seventeenth century, there were very few punctuation marks. English was so heavily influenced by Latin we didn't need them. Then the novel was invented. That changed everything. Writing styles moved more toward the way we talk and away from the way scholars thought writing should be. The punctuation marks we use today were invented to make Latin-constructed sentences sound the way English people speak.

Today there are over 30 punctuation marks. Fortunately, we don't regularly use more than 10 or 12 of them, but a few of these 10 or 12 give us more trouble than all the ones we don't use put together.

Here are two guidelines to follow when wrestling with punctuation:

If you're not sure what to do, don't do anything.

If you're going to do something, have a reason.

Even the strictest grammarian can find a reason why you might leave out a punctuation mark, but to put one in where it doesn't belong is to be wrong every single time.

Because punctuation marks are as much a part of our written language as words, the conventions that govern punctuation are just as inconsistent, contradictory, and evolving. The purpose of this book is not to resolve these differences but to make you aware of the most common usages.

THE PERIOD

The *period* means "Stop. Take a breath of air." The capital letter of the first word of the next sentence means "Go." The easiest to use and most popular punctuation mark, the period instills in us the most confidence. We know how to use it. So use it. Often. It helps keep your sentences short and eliminates the kinds of punctuation problems that result from constructing longer, more elaborately designed sentences.

Periods are also used:

- In abbreviations (9 a.m., U.S.A., Prof. Ken Washington, i.e.), but many abbreviations no longer contain periods, especially the abbreviations of names of agencies, corporations, and colleges (CIA, IBM, UCLA).

- After numerals or letters preceding listed items.

- With decimals.

Don't use periods:

- In acronyms.

- After displayed headings.

- After listed items that aren't complete sentences.

Compare the following list:

Successful meetings have the following four characteristics:

1. An agenda that is distributed in advance

2. A meeting leader who keeps the meeting moving

3. Participants who come prepared

4. Someone who follows up on tasks that are assigned to meeting participants

To this one:

Successful meetings share several characteristics, including:

1. An agenda that is distributed in advance.

2. A meeting leader who keeps the meeting moving.

3. Participants who come prepared.

4. Someone who follows up on tasks that are assigned to meeting participants.

Notice that the items in the second list form a grammatically correct sentence with the introductory phrase; therefore, each item is punctuated with a period.

THE QUESTION MARK

The *question mark*:

- Indicates that a question has been asked.

  Did you ask that question?

- Indicates doubt.

  The university hasn't graduated a single basketball player in the last 10 years?

81

THE EXCLAMATION POINT

The *exclamation point* intensifies the urgency or importance of a message.

Use them sparingly! Too many will weaken your message! People won't share your intensity! They won't respond! You won't get what you want!

THE COMMA

The *comma* means "pause," but it also makes clear the syntax of any sentence. It tells us how the words are meant to be received and understood. Here are the major rules governing the comma:

- Commas separate two sentences joined by a conjunction.

   William Carlos Williams was a poet, and he was also a doctor who made house calls.

- Commas separate introductory phrases and clauses from the main parts of sentences.

   In addition to being a poet, William Carlos Williams was a doctor who made house calls.

There are some who say the comma can be eliminated if the introductory phrase or clause is short:

   After today William Carlos Williams will be well known.

Although some people say you can leave the comma out, you'll never be wrong and you'll always be safe if you put it in. Notice, for example, what happens to us as readers when the writer leaves out a comma after *publishing* in the next sentence:

   Before publishing his first works were in journals.

- Commas separate items in a series.

    William Carlos Williams was a doctor, a poet, and a critic of American literature.

Here, too, there is a movement to leave the comma out after *poet* and before *and*. That's because the comma was created to take the place of *and*, so to include it is redundant.

And, once again, fashion collides with sense. In the previous example about William Carlos Williams, to leave the comma out does not cause confusion, but what about this sentence:

    The jars contained apples, strawberries and rhubarb and peaches.

Did some of the jars contain apples, some strawberries, some rhubarb, and some peaches? Or did some contain apples and some a mixture of strawberry and rhubarb? Or some apples, some strawberries, and some rhubarb and peaches? In a recent legal case in Illinois, a lawyer convinced a judge to divide an estate two ways rather than three because of the absence of a comma. Moral? You'll never be wrong and you'll always be safe if you put the comma in.

Taking out the comma after short introductory phrases and clauses and eliminating it before *and* when listing items in a series reflects the influence of journalism. Newspapers are always looking for ways to create space for advertising—their real business. They'll even go so far as to remove letters from words. The *Washington Post*, for example, decided recently that the second *e* in *employee* is unnecessary. But the paper received so many letters pointing out that its editors didn't know how to spell *employee*, that the full spelling of the word has since been reinstated.

- Commas separate phrases and clauses that aren't a part of the main sentence.

    The teacher, a leader in her field, wants to help people help themselves.

The school, which is in the business of helping people help themselves, is a leader in its field.

- Commas separate adjectives in a series.

    This is a simple, clear, understandable book.

    But not always. Take, for example, the phrase *three blind mice*. You wouldn't put a comma between *three* and *blind*. To determine when a comma is needed to separate adjectives in a series, substitute the word *and* for each of your commas. If the sentence still makes sense after you include the word *and*, the commas are needed. If the sentence doesn't make sense (*three and blind mice*), then remove the comma.

- Commas separate what is being said from who is saying it.

    Mark Twain said, "Golf is a good walk spoiled."

    "I never let school interfere with my education," Mark Twain once said.

- Commas separate transitional words from the rest of the sentence.

    Furthermore, she was always right.

    He, however, was never wrong.

    They, moreover, couldn't agree.

    Nevertheless, they got married.

- Commas separate the names of people addressed in a sentence.

    Well, Steve, we finally won a game.

- Commas separate titles and degrees from the names they're associated with.

    Jess Bessinger, Ph.D., will discuss his work on the Sutton Hoo exhibit.

    Connie Hall, executive vice president, wrote a memo addressing the issue of overtime pay.

- Commas separate items in dates, addresses, and geographical locations.

    She comes from Athens, Greece.

    Her proposal was submitted on May 21, 1992.

    The client's address is 555 Westover Avenue, Citytown, Kansas.

One of the most common errors involving the comma is the *comma splice*. A comma splice occurs when we use only a comma to separate two sentences when we should use a period, a semicolon, or a comma and a conjunction. Here's an example of a comma splice error:

    Mary mailed the record, John played it.

This sentence could be rewritten in any of the following ways:

    Mary mailed the record. John played it.

    Mary mailed the record; John played it.

    Mary mailed the record, and John played it.

Note that the comma splice error is so common it is used by many respected writers—Margaret Atwood and Margaret Drabble to name two—on the ground that it makes any sentence read faster. "John hit the ball, he ran to first" conveys a greater sense of the action than any conventionally punctuated form. Until the comma splice gains wider acceptance, however, play it safe and stick to the standard.

THE COLON

The *colon* is used to:

- Introduce something that explains or illustrates what has come before it.

    This is the purpose of our mission: to win.

- Introduce a list or a series of examples.

    There are three steps to writing successful memos and letters: think, write, and correct.

However, do *not* use a colon to separate a series that flows grammatically with the rest of the sentence, unless you present those items as a list on separate lines. Compare this sentence:

> The three steps to writing successful memos and letters are thinking, writing, and correcting.

to this one that requires a colon before the series of items:

> The three steps to writing successful memos and letters are:
>
> 1. Thinking.
>
> 2. Writing.
>
> 3. Correcting.

- Separate subtitles from titles.

  Fictions of Authority: Women Writers and Narrative Voice

- Introduce quotations that are more than three lines long.

- End a salutation in formal correspondence.

THE SEMICOLON

The *semicolon* can:

- Separate two sentences.

  William Carlos Williams was a poet; he was also a doctor.

- Separate two sentences joined by connecting words such as *however*, *but*, *consequently*, and *thus*.

  William Carlos Williams was a poet; however, he was also a doctor.

The careful writer follows these rules on the grounds that tradition frowns on beginning a sentence with *but* or *however*. Nevertheless, an increasing number of writers regularly begin their sentences with these linking words and require the semicolon only *to separate items in a series that include commas.*

> Henry Kissinger reported on weather conditions in Rome, New York; Lebanon, Pennsylvania; and Paris, Texas.

THE APOSTROPHE

The *apostrophe* has two major uses.

- The apostrophe takes the place of missing letters in contractions.

> It's a breeze.
>
> You can't do that.
>
> Wouldn't you like to know.

Note that *it's* is a contraction for *it is; it's* is also a contraction for *it has. It's* is never used to show the possessive case of *it.* The possessive case of *it* is written *its.*

- The apostrophe indicates possession.

> The boy's bag was large.
>
> The boys' bags were large.
>
> The boss's desk is clean.
>
> The bosses' desks are clean.

Note that when the possessive word is singular, the apostrophe comes before the *s*; when the possessive word is plural, the apostrophe comes after the *s*.

The major exceptions to this rule are men, women, children, and people.

The men's lockers were full.

The women's books were left at the door.

The children's toys arrived in time.

The people's vote didn't count.

Another exception is people's names ending in *s*. With some names, we add an *'s*; with others we just add an apostrophe.

Charles's desk is messy.

We went to Jerry Mathers' house.

Although we generally add an *'s* to first names ending in *s* and add only an apostrophe to last names ending in *s*, the key for choosing correctly is sound. If when we speak a person's name, we add the *s* after the apostrophe, then we also add the *s* when we write that person's name. On the other hand, if we don't add the *s* when we speak, we leave it out when we write and just add the apostrophe.

The apostrophe also shows possession for *pairs* of nouns. The rule here is to use *'s* after the second noun:

Joe and Tom's account

The father and mother's interest

However, if your intention is to show individual possession rather than joint possession, use an *s* after both nouns:

Joe's and Tom's accounts

- The apostrophe is used to indicate a quote within a quote.

Mary said, "Put all the pop cans in the bin marked 'Recyclables.'"

- The apostrophe is sometimes used to indicate the plurals of single letters, numbers, and time periods.

    1990's

    the three R's

    Although style books disagree about whether to use the apostrophe in these instances, always be consistent within the same piece of writing.

QUOTATION MARKS

Several rules govern the use of *quotation marks*. Here are a few basic ones to remember:

- Quotation marks identify direct quotations.

    Mary said, "Bring me the pen."

    Note that indirect quotes do not require quotation marks.

    Mary said to bring the pen. (indirect quotation)

- Quotation marks identify titles of works that can be placed within a larger context.

    "Punctuation" is the title of this chapter.

    Note that quotation marks enclose titles of poems, short stories, and articles. The titles of the larger texts in which these works appear are underlined or placed in italics.

    "Taxes: You Gotta Love 'Em" appears in this week's issue of *The Valley Advocate.*

- Quotation marks indicate words that are used in an ironical sense:

    My "vacation" turned into a nightmare.

Quotation marks often appear with other punctuation marks. In Great Britain, writers place these other punctuation marks either inside the quotation marks or outside of them depending on whether the punctuation mark is part of the quotation. In the United States, however, the common practice is to:

- Place periods and commas inside the quotation marks.

- Place colons and semicolons outside the quotation marks.

Even when it makes sense not to.

Exclamation points, question marks, and dashes follow the British convention. They go inside or outside of the quotation marks depending on whether they are part of the quotation.

THE DASH

The *dash*—once the rage in the nineteenth century and discarded at the beginning of the twentieth for being overdone—is back. Today, it is the all-purpose punctuation mark. An effective way to emphasize points or call attention to specific information, the dash can be used to:

- Connect thoughts to the beginning or end of a sentence.

   "What made Mickey Mantle great was he could hit just as good right-handed as he could left-handed—he's naturally amphibious."
   Yogi Berra

- Take the place of colons.

   This is the purpose of our mission—to win.

- Insert a thought into a sentence.

   "Stopping otter hunting—a possible issue for the Sierra Club—is unlikely to benefit otters."
   Field Magazine

- To add information to some word, phrase, or clause in a sentence.

> "Fishing—and I can only compare it to a stick and a string with a worm at one end and a fool at the other—is something I've never done."
>
> Dr. Samuel Johnson

Note that the dash—made by typing two unspaced hyphens on a typewriter or a special code on a word processor—has no space between it and the words it links.

6

THE SLASH

In business writing, a slash, sometimes called a virgule, can mean "and," "or," "either one," and "both." In each of these cases, the slash is best avoided.

Take, for example, this sentence:

> We want a refund and/or a voucher for another meal at your restaurant.

Does this sentence mean we want a refund *and* a voucher or a refund *or* a voucher? The use of *and/or* makes the meaning ambiguous.

PARENTHESES

Parentheses, like commas and dashes, can be used to add information to a sentence. Which pair you use depends on the amount of attention you want your reader to pay to the inserted information. If your inserted information is separated from the rest of the sentence by commas, your reader will pause slightly before and after each comma. Dashes create a slightly longer pause, and the reader will pay slightly more attention to what you've inserted. Parentheses slow the reader down most of all but, because parentheses have also been used to indicate that the enclosed reading is optional, readers tend not to pay as close attention to what has been inserted. Dashes, then, state their messages more emphatically than parentheses.

Parentheses can be used to:

- Explain.

    The thought (that he might win) came in the middle of the night.

- Refer.

    Van Gogh's "Room at Arles" (see figure 45) currently hangs at the Musee D'Orsay.

- Enclose the abbreviations or acronyms of spelled-out forms, or vice versa.

    The National Association for the Advancement of Colored People (NAACP) increased its membership this year.

- Indicate the source of information within text.

    Recent studies (Lawson, 1991) show that economic predictions are unreliable.

Note that if a whole sentence is enclosed by parentheses, the period goes inside of the closing parenthesis. If only part of a sentence is enclosed by parentheses, the period goes outside of the closing parenthesis.

(See Van Gogh, "Room at Arles," figure 45.)

Van Gogh painted this room in an asylum two months before he killed himself (see Van Gogh, "Room at Arles," figure 45).

THE HYPHEN

The *hyphen* connects:

- Compound nouns.

    My mother-in-law is visiting us.

    Self-awareness is an important issue.

- Compound verbs.

    Double-space that report.

    Have him re-sign the contract.

- Compound adjectives.

    She has the decision-making authority.

    His matter-of-fact approach has helped.

    Her focus is on twentieth-century literature.

Unfortunately, not all compound words are hyphenated. And sometimes a compound word will require a hyphen and other times it will not. Whether or not to use the hyphen in these instances depends largely on whether the prefix forms a word that has a different meaning.

    Please re-cover the typewriter.

    Will you recover soon?

Use common sense and your dictionary to determine your choice.

The hyphen also:

- Indicates a suspension between the first and subsequent words in a hyphenated compound.

    The engineer submitted a report describing the differences between the low- and high-performance engine models.

6

- Separates the numerator from the denominator in spelled-out fractions.

  one-third

  three-fourths

- Divides a word of more than two syllables at the end of a line.

  "The taste of defeat has a richness of experience all its own."

  Bill Bradley

To maintain a professional appearance in your memo or letter:

- Avoid ending more than two consecutive lines with hyphens.

- Avoid ending the first and last lines of paragraphs with hyphens.

- Avoid dividing a line-ending word after only one syllable. Put the whole word on the next line.

- Avoid hyphenating the last word on a page. Move the whole word to the next page.

BRACKETS

Because *brackets* are most often used to take the place of parentheses and because many typewriters and some word processors lack the ability to indicate brackets, we can avoid them almost altogether.

The "almost" is on that rare occasion when you need to enclose some explanatory material within a statement that is already separated from the rest of the sentence by parentheses.

> Though it was lower than we had hoped, we accepted the bid on our house (the closest bid [$120,000] was still $10,000 less than the highest one offered) because we were in a hurry to move.

As you can see, once you begin using brackets and parentheses in the same sentence, you start bordering on the unintelligible. When you find yourself wrestling with brackets and parentheses, consider rewriting the sentence.

> Even though the $120,000 bid was less than we hoped, we accepted it because we were in a hurry to move and it was still $10,000 higher than the other bids we received.

ELLIPSES

Ellipses are comprised of three spaced periods (. . .) and indicate:

- Words that are left out of a quoted sentence.

> "Fans are people who would if they could but they can't . . . so they tell those who can how they should."
>> Steve Tuck

- Speech that is faltering.

> "Do you think . . . perhaps . . . I could have a minute of your time . . . if you're not too busy, I mean."

- In advertising, a series of words that are usually separated by a comma.

> Office space with . . . a great view . . . convenient parking . . . easy highway access . . .

A FINAL WORD ABOUT PUNCTUATION

Even grammar guides disagree about punctuation. That's because punctuation rules and styles change over time. Remember, the *clarity* of your message is always more important than any "rules" of punctuation. But whichever form you use, be consistent!

6

Syntax

S yntax is the way we construct our phrases, clauses, and sentences. Some syntaxes—depending on the reader and the situation—are more effective than others. All syntax errors, however, undermine our credibility. The most common stumbling blocks are *agreement* and *modifiers*.

AGREEMENT

Agreement means that the specific use of some words in a sentence re-quires the specific use of other words. For example, the use of the word *he* or *she* in a sentence requires the form *has* of the verb *to be*:

He <u>has</u> 10 minutes to file the report.

We cannot say:

He <u>have</u> 10 minutes to file the report.

There are two kinds of agreement errors. Together they make up the majority of our syntax errors. The first kind is *subject-verb agreement*; the second kind is *noun-pronoun agreement*.

Subject-Verb Agreement

The rule is that singular subjects require singular verbs and plural subjects require plural verbs. We all know this rule and can match correctly any number of given nouns and verbs. Problems occur, however, when we write a singular subject; then, before we write our verb, we write a few more words. By the time we're ready to write our verb, we've forgotten the subject. Or rather, the subject is now far enough away from where we started that we make our verb agree with the last word that came into our minds rather than with the subject of the sentence. The following example makes clear why this is the most common of all grammatical mistakes.

A collection of stamps <u>are</u> on display.

The subject of this sentence is *collection*. If asked to choose between *collection is* or *collection are*, we would invariably choose *collection is*. When the word *stamps* comes between the verb and the subject *collection*, however, we—without thinking—make the verb agree with the last word we wrote rather than with the word it refers to. The correct syntax for this sentence is:

A collection of stamps <u>is</u> on display.

Here are some other examples of subject-verb agreement errors. Notice how, in each case, the writer makes the verb agree with the word that comes before it rather than with the subject of the sentence.

The board's <u>members</u>, one of whom is a student, <u>meets</u> tonight.

The writer made *meets* agree with the last word that came into his or her mind *(student)* instead of with the word it should agree with *(members)*.

Incorrect: Only one of the issues <u>are</u> . . .

Correct: Only one of the issues <u>is</u> . . .

Incorrect: Few parts of the puzzle <u>is</u> . . .

Correct: Few parts of the puzzle <u>are</u> . . .

To correct problems in subject-verb agreement, practice the *Two-Finger Exercise*. Place one finger of your left hand on the subject of the sentence, place one finger of your right hand on the verb, and ask yourself this question: "Do these two words agree in number?" By isolating the two words and reading them aloud, you will know immediately which form of the verb you have to choose to make it agree with your subject.

Noun-Pronoun Agreement

The rule is that pronouns must agree in number, gender, and person with the nouns they take the place of.

Gender: <u>Mike</u> was eager to begin <u>his</u> interview.

Number: The <u>women</u> completed <u>their</u> tasks first.

The problem occurs when we use an indefinite pronoun as the subject of our sentence. Because the pronoun is *indefinite*, we're often not sure what number it is or whether it is masculine or feminine.

Many indefinite pronouns (*each, anyone, everyone, everybody, someone,* and *none*) are considered singular and traditionally require singular pronouns even if both sexes are represented. The most common example of this is:

<u>Everyone</u> should submit <u>his</u> report.

Because sexist writing is no longer acceptable, the construction

<u>Everyone</u> should submit <u>their</u> report.

has become increasingly more acceptable as an alternative to the awkward-sounding:

Everyone should submit his or her report.

To avoid offending either the traditionalists or the enlightened, however, consider changing every pronoun to the plural.

All should submit their reports.

For other gender-free alternatives to awkward constructions, consult Chapter 4 on word usage.

Here is a list of the most common indefinite pronouns requiring singular agreement:

another	everyone	nothing
anybody	everybody	one
anyone	everything	somebody
anything	much	someone
each	neither	something
either	nobody	
every	no one	

Here is a list of the most common indefinite pronouns requiring plural agreement:

both	many	several
few	others	

Some indefinite pronouns may be singular or plural, depending on the noun they refer to. Note that *none* is considered a singular pronoun in formal writing but not in general usage.

all	more	none
any	most	some

MODIFIERS

Modifiers are words or groups of words that describe or limit other words. In the phrase *the red book*, the word *red* is a modifier because it describes the book's color. *Until I find my keys*, acts as a modifier in the sentence *Until I find my keys, we're not going anywhere* because it limits the time of departure.

Most adjective modifiers come in front of the words they modify, and most adjective phrases come after the words they modify. Adverb modifiers and adverbial phrases have been given greater freedom in sentences because their meanings are more clear. As a general guideline, however, you may wish to keep all your words and phrases as close as possible to the words they modify.

The two most common modifier mistakes are *misplaced modifiers* and *dangling modifiers*.

Misplaced Modifiers

A *misplaced modifier* appears to modify a word other than the one intended.

A <u>manuscript</u> was discovered in Sweden <u>that was thought to be lost</u>.

Wasn't Sweden there the last time we looked?

She <u>almost</u> understood every word.

Half-understanding isn't half-bad, is it?

All the people were born in September <u>in this room</u>.

Big room.

These sentences should read:

A manuscript that was lost was discovered in Sweden.

She understood almost every word.

All the people in this room were born in September.

Dangling Modifiers

A *dangling modifier* is one that has no doer.

Walking down the aisle, the typewriters make a lot of noise.

With those shoes, it's no wonder!

Having missed our exam, no make-ups were being given.

Who missed this exam?

These sentences should read:

Walking down the aisle, I heard the typewriters make a lot of noise.

After missing our exam, we discovered that no make-ups were being given.

Even though agreement and modifiers are the most common syntax errors, there are some other common constructions that cause problems every time we encounter them.

WHO VS. WHOM

There are three reasons why *who* and *whom* give us so much trouble:

1. We rarely use *whom*.

2. When we use *whom*, the sentence is often in a kind of inverted order that sounds unnatural.

3. When the sentence is in an inverted order, we have difficulty determining whether the *who* or *whom* serves as the subject of a verb or the object of a verb or preposition.

To solve this problem, look at the word following your choice of *who* or *whom*. If the next word in the sentence is a verb or an adverb, your choice *almost always* will be *who*. If the next word in the sentence is not a verb or an adverb, your choice almost always will be *whom*.

> <u>Who/Whom</u> wants this job?

Since the word after your choice is a verb, chances are the word you want is *who*.

> Michael, <u>who/whom</u> the university is considering for the position, is out of town.

Because the word after your choice is a not a verb or an adverb, the word you're looking for is *whom*.

I VS. ME

Our parents are to blame for this one. Remember telling them, "Mary and me are going to the store"? And remember being told, "Mary and *I* are going to the store"?

Because of the constant correcting, we learned to use *I* whenever coupling ourselves with someone else in a sentence.

> Bring the letter to <u>Mary and I</u>.

As correct as this may sound, *Mary and I* are the objects of the preposition *to*, so you need to use the objective form of the pronoun. The sentence should read:

> Bring the letter to <u>Mary and me</u>.

To determine the correct use of *I* when coupled with another person in the sentence, cover with one finger the name of the other person. Then read the sentence once with the word *I* and once with the word *me*. Whichever sentence sounds correct will be correct.

Bring the letter to I.

Bring the letter to me.

The correct choice is obvious.

EITHER/OR AND NEITHER/NOR

There are a number of rules governing *either/or* and *neither/nor*, but there is only one you have to remember and only one exception to it.

The rule:

Make your verb agree in number with the noun that follows the *or* or *nor*.

Either the boy or the girl wants it.

Neither the boy nor the girl wants it.

Either the boys or the girls want it.

Neither the boys nor the girls want it.

Either the boys (plural) or the girl (singular) wants it.

Neither the boy (singular) nor the girls (plural) want it.

The exception:

When the word *one* is not written in the sentence but is *understood* to be included, the verb is singular.

Neither (one) wants it.

Neither (one) of the boys wants it.

ACTIVE VOICE VS. PASSIVE VOICE

A verb is in the *active voice* when the subject of the sentence is doing the action:

> John read the report.

Passive voice occurs when the action is being done to the subject.

> The report was read by John.

The problem with passive voice is that it slows the reader down. Five or six passive-voice constructions in a row and the reader tires. Unless you're covering something up (a mistake was made, and we don't know who's responsible) or trying to spare the feelings of the person who made the mistake (an error was found, and you have to do something about it), active voice is almost always the shorter, simpler, clearer way to go. It's the more effective way to keep our readers engaged in the subjects of our memos and letters.

7

RULES THAT ARE NO LONGER RULES

Many of the conventions we follow as rules didn't start out as rules. They started out as suggestions. But because we're so insecure about our writing, we've taken some of these suggestions and shackled ourselves by turning them into rules. Every suggestion turned into a rule is another limitation on the ways we have of expressing what we want to say. Here are some "rules" that are no longer adhered to as strictly as they once were:

- *Ending a sentence with a preposition.* Thanks to Winston Churchill, we can now end our sentences with prepositions. When asked if he ever ended a sentence with a preposition, Churchill replied, "Ending a sentence with a preposition is something up with which I will not put." He made us realize what a silly rule this is. If we can end our sentences in prepositions when we speak, we can also end our sentences with prepositions when we write.

This rule began as a suggestion in the eighteenth century when writers were trying to discover the most powerful ways to end their sentences. One of their conclusions was that nouns and verbs made more powerful endings than any other parts of speech. What started out as a suggestion got turned into a rule by insecure writers.

More often than not, it is more effective to write the natural-sounding "I'm the one you spoke to" and end a sentence with a preposition than search around for the more grammatically correct but awkward and artificial-sounding "I'm the one to whom you spoke."

- *Beginning a sentence with a conjunction.* Again, this practice grew out of the influence of journalists trying to create advertising space by eliminating words they think are unnecessary.

While it is true that many times the *and* or *but* that we use to begin a sentence isn't necessary and that eliminating it doesn't change the meaning of the sentence, there are some times when we want to begin our sentences with a conjunction.

Beginning a sentence with *and* or *but* or some other conjunction often adds emphasis to our message. For example:

> We shall fight them on the beaches, we shall fight them on the shores, we shall fight them in the villages and the streets. And we shall never surrender.

Sometimes, the sentence that comes before the one beginning with a conjunction requires that the conjunction be retained. For example:

> Everyone got their money in on time. But not us.

- *Splitting an infinitive.* An *infinitive* is the word *to* followed by a verb, as in *to run, to ski, to sleep,* and *to read.* We were taught never to split an infinitive, never to put any words between the *to* and the verb that follows it. Following that rule, how else would you say:

> You're going to really enjoy that movie.

To write these grammatically correct sentences is to sound awkward and risk distancing your reader from your message:

> You're going to enjoy really that movie.
>
> You're going really to enjoy that movie.

- *Using the word "I" in a business letter.* Another good suggestion turned into an undermining rule. The original suggestion was that most people in business don't care about the writer; they only care about themselves. So the original idea was to try to create "reader-centered" rather than "writer-centered" prose.

  Somehow, this turned into "Never use the word *I*."

  There are times when the subjects of our letters require that we use *I*. Complaint letters, for example. When we write a complaint letter, we want our readers to see things from our point of view, to understand and sympathize with what happened to us, to do something for us. Using the word *I* is the most seductive technique writers have for encouraging their readers to see everything from the writers' points of view. Using the word *you* in a complaint letter makes your readers feel responsible for what happened to you; it makes them want to distance themselves from your point of view, become defensive, and argue against you.

  Using the word *I* is not only acceptable in today's business letters, it's also effective. But what's the best way to provide "reader-centered" prose? Compose every rough draft the natural way—from your own point of view. Then, once you have the words on the page, edit them as best you can into the reader's point of view. Cross out some of the *I*'s that came naturally; see how many of them you can change to *you*; determine how many *I*'s you want to leave as they are because you think their use is the most effective way to convey your message.

- *Repeating words.* There's some truth to this. Repeating the same word can create an echo effect in a memo or letter. The other side of the truth is that is that by repeating some words, our messages become even more powerful. Imagine Abraham Lincoln writing:

That this government of the people, by the persons, and for all the men, women, and children shall not perish from the earth.

A FINAL WORD ON RULES

The rules of grammar were created to make our lives easier, but we only make our lives more difficult when we try to compile a list of commandments all beginning with *Don't* in the hope that if we obey these commandments, we won't make any grammatical mistakes.

You no longer have to obey rules that were never rules to begin with, and you can break *any* grammatical rule if you do it right. By "do it right," we mean that you know what you're doing and your readers know what you're doing. Then your writing becomes even more powerful by breaking the rule.

For example:

Nobody beats Midas. Nobody.

That second *nobody* is a sentence fragment. It's not a complete thought. Take it away, however, and you rob the message of most of its power.

And it works because the reader understands what the writer has done.

A FINAL WORD ON SYNTAX

For most of the history of the English language, there has been a battle raging between the rules and the language. Except for certain slang words—ones that are popular for only a short period of time—the language almost always wins.

Our language is loaded with words and expressions that mean something very different from what they were intended to mean. Some of our expressions don't even make grammatical sense. But because we all agree on what we mean by these words and expressions, they become acceptable.

The word *terrific*, for example, comes from *terrify*, but to use *terrific* in the original sense would confuse our readers. You can look it up. *You can look it up* doesn't make grammatical sense, but the syntax is acceptable because we all use it.

For this reason, rely on your ears when it comes to most matters of syntax. Syntax almost always follows the patterns set by the spoken language. To test the correct syntax of any sentence, read it aloud. If it *sounds* right, it probably is. If you're still not sure, read your sentence to someone else. Their objective set of ears will tell you what you need to know. They may not be able to tell you what's wrong with the sentence, but they'll know—just from hearing it—whether it's right or not.

7

Mechanics

Mechanics, like their close relative *spelling* and their distant cousin *punctuation*, deal almost exclusively with the written rather than the spoken language. When we speak, we don't worry about whether our sentences begin with a capital letter. When we write, however, we have to make sure every sentence begins with a capital letter. And so must a lot of other things.

What makes mechanics difficult is their general lack of flexibility. Most of the time, the writer is either right or wrong. There is little room for the kind of individual expression that's available in syntax.

CAPITALIZATION

Capitalize the first letter of:

- *Sentences.*

    Your clothes are ready.

- *Lines of traditional poetry.*

  <u>R</u>oses are red; violets are blue.
  <u>M</u>ost poems rhyme; this one doesn't.

- *Listed items.*

  The following topics will be discussed:

  <u>S</u>alary increases

  <u>P</u>ension plans

  <u>H</u>ealth benefits

- *The first word and all the main words in titles of:*

Books:	*<u>M</u>oby <u>D</u>ick*
Plays:	*<u>L</u>ook <u>B</u>ack in <u>A</u>nger*
Movies:	*<u>M</u>arathon <u>M</u>an*
Articles:	"<u>D</u>ead <u>M</u>all <u>G</u>oes <u>W</u>holesale"
Essays:	"<u>H</u>ow to <u>B</u>uy a <u>H</u>ome"
Poems:	"<u>T</u>he <u>R</u>aven"
Short stories:	"<u>A</u> Rose for <u>E</u>mily"

- *The first word and all the main words of headings, salutations, and subject lines.*

  <u>P</u>arking <u>R</u>egulations

  <u>D</u>ear <u>S</u>ir or <u>M</u>adam:

- *The first word of closings.*

  <u>Y</u>ours truly,

  <u>S</u>incerely yours,

- *Names of people.*

  John F. Kennedy

  Martin Luther King, Jr.

- *Names of places.*

  New York

  France

- *Names of schools.*

  University of Illinois

  Harvard University

- *Names of religions.*

  Roman Catholic

  Greek Orthodox

- *Names of organizations.*

  Exxon Corporation

  United Negro College Fund

- *Names of races.*

  Asian

  Caucasian

- *Names of nationalities.*

  German

  Japanese

8

- *Names of geographical regions when they refer to a definite region or are part of a proper name.*

  Midwest

  South

  the Far East

  But, do not capitalize these words when they indicate direction or refer to a general location.

  The corporate offices are located 2 miles south of the highway.

- *Names of one-of-a-kind events.*

  World War I

  Industrial Revolution

- *Names of the months and holidays.*

  December

  Fourth of July

- *Names of brands.*

  Coca-Cola

  Kleenex

- *Names of people's titles or positions when they precede the people's names.*

  Personnel Director Alisa Harper

  but:

  Alisa Harper, personnel director, processed applications for the accounting position.

Prof. Thomas

but:

Edward Thomas, professor, will retire at the end of the semester.

Vice President Keith Miller announced the company's relocation.

but:

Keith Miller, vice president, announced the company's relocation.

- *Single letters when part of a name.*

    A-frame

    vitamin C

- *Names of departments within a company or organization for internal communications (follow your company's policy).*

    The Accounting Department won this year's United Way drive.

    Usually, when you are referring to a department in another company, you will lowercase the department name.

    Our competitor's research department is experimenting with a new adhesive backing for its labels.

ABBREVIATIONS

Abbreviations are the shortened forms of words. Both useful and widely used in informal writing, they've become increasingly more acceptable in formal writing. The great advantage of abbreviations is that they save us from having to repeat lengthy words and phrases.

The most important things to remember when using abbreviations are to make sure your reader understands them and to use them consistently within a document.

8

Most abbreviations fall into one of two categories: those to use and those not to use.

1. Abbreviations to use:

- *Personal titles*

    <u>Mr.</u> Francis

    <u>Dr.</u> Francis

    <u>Prof.</u> Francis

    <u>Ms.</u> Francis

    <u>Mrs.</u> Francis

    <u>St.</u> Francis

- Junior *and* senior

    John Francis, <u>Jr.</u>

- *Professional titles after a full personal name*

    John Francis, <u>Ph.D.</u>

    Mary Francis, <u>M.D.</u>

- *Time and temperature*

    10:30 <u>a.m.</u> or 10:30 <u>A.M</u>

    11:30 <u>EST</u>

    <u>A.D.</u> 734

    734 <u>B.C.</u>

- The word *number* when accompanied by a numeral

    Train <u>No.</u> 55 will arrive on Track <u>No.</u> 7.

    Flight <u>No.</u> 1 will depart from Gate <u>No.</u> 3.

2. Abbreviations to avoid:

- *Names of people*

    <u>Robt.</u> Browning was a poet.

- *Names of geographical locations*

    March up <u>Bdwy.</u>

- *Names of countries, states, and cities in formal writing.* It's okay to use these abbreviations in addresses or tables or charts.

    I went to school in <u>L.A., Calif.</u>

Note that a single period is used when an abbreviation ends a sentence. You don't need to use a period both for the abbreviation and to end the sentence.

- *Names of months, days, and holidays*

    She was born on <u>Sept. 19, 1961.</u>

8

Common Abbreviations

Note: Since the United States Post Office reduced the abbreviations of all states to two letters and eliminated all periods (VT, CA, FL, CO), many people have begun capitalizing all the letters in their abbreviations and dropping all the periods. Today, the abbreviation for Internal Revenue Service can be written as either *I.R.S.* or *IRS*. Even the previously untouched *a.m.* and *p.m.* now appear occasionally as *AM* and *PM*.

AA	Alcoholics Anonymous
abbr.	abbreviation
acct.	account
ACLU	American Civil Liberties Union
A.D.	(*Anno Domini*) in the year of the Lord
agt.	agent
a.k.a.	also known as
a.m.	(*ante meridiem*) before noon
AM	amplitude modulation
AMA	American Medical Association
Amb.	ambassador
AP	Associated Press
ASAP	as soon as possible
assoc.	association
Attn.	Attention
atty.	attorney
aux.	auxiliary
Ave.	avenue
AWOL	absent without leave

Common Abbreviations

B.A.	Bachelor of Arts
bbl	barrel
bbl/d	barrel per day
B.C.	before Christ
BLS	Bureau of Labor Statistics
Blvd.	boulevard
B.S.	Bachelor of Science
C	Celsius
cc	carbon copy
CD	compact disc
chap.	chapter
CIA	Central Intelligence Agency
cm	centimeter
Co.	company
cont.	continued
Corp.	corporation
CPA	certified public accountant
CPI	consumer price index
CPR	cardiopulmonary resuscitation
crit.	criticism
CSC	Civil Service Commission
CST	Central standard time
ctr.	center
d	date
DAR	Daughters of the American Revolution

8

Common Abbreviations

DBA or d.b.a.	doing business as
D.D.	Doctor of Divinity
D.D.S.	Doctor of Dental Surgery
diag.	diagram
Dist. Ct.	District Court
ditto	the same
dob	date of birth
doz.	dozen
Dr.	doctor
D.V.M.	Doctor of Veterinary Medicine
E.	east
Ed.D.	Doctor of Education
edit.	editor, edited, edition
e.g.	(*exempli gratia*) for example
EKG	electrocardiogram
emcee	master of ceremony
enc.	enclosure
EST	Eastern standard time
et al.	(*et alii*) and others
etc.	(*et cetera*) and others
ex lib	(*ex libris*) from the books of
F	Fahrenheit
FAA	Federal Aviation Agency
FBI	Federal Bureau of Investigation
FCC	Federal Communications Commission

FDA	Food and Drug Administration
FDIC	Federal Deposit Insurance Corporation
Fed.	federal
fem.	feminine
FHA	Federal Housing Administration
FM	frequency modulation
f.o.b. or FOB	free on board
Fr.	Father (priest)
ft	foot
FYI	for your information
gal	gallon
G.A.O.	General Accounting Office
GNP	gross national product
GOP	Grand Old Party (Republican Party)
Gov.	governor
govt or Govt	government
gr. wt.	gross weight
grad.	graduate
hdqrs.	headquarters
HEW	Department of Health, Education, and Welfare
HP or hp	horsepower
hr	hour
ibid.	(*ibidem*) in the same place
id.	(*idem*) the same
i.e.	(*id est*) that is

8

Common Abbreviations

illus.	illustrated
in	inch
Inc.	incorporated
ind.	independent
IQ	intelligence quotient
IRS	Internal Revenue Service
Is.	island
J.D.	(*jurim doctor*) doctor of laws
JP	Justice of the Peace
Jr.	junior
k	kilo; thousand (4k=4,000)
K. of C.	Knights of Columbus
kg	kilogram
km	kilometer
kn	knot
kw	kilowatt
l	liter
lb	pound
LL.B.	Bachelor of Laws
LL.D.	Doctor of Laws
Ltd.	limited
m	meter
masc.	masculine
M.D.	Doctor of Medicine
memo	memorandum

Common Abbreviations	mg	milogram
	min	minute
	M.O.	(*modus operandi*) way of operating
	mph	miles per hour
	Mr.	mister
	Mrs.	mistress
	Ms.	standard for addressing women
	MS or ms	manuscript
	M.S.	Master of Science
	Mses.	plural of Ms.
	Msgr.	monsignor
	MSS or mss	manuscripts
	MST	Mountain standard time
	myth	mythology
	N.	north
	NA	not available
	NAACP	Nation Association for the Advancement of Colored People
	NASA	National Aeronautics and Space Administration
	natl	national
	NATO	North Atlantic Treaty Organization
	N.B.	(*nota bene*) note well
	N.E.	northeast
	ng	no good
	No.	number

8

Mechanics

Common Abbreviations

nt. wt.	net weight
N.W.	northwest
OK	okay
oz	ounce
PA	public address system
PC	personal computer
pct.	percent
Ph.D.	Doctor of Philosophy
PIN	personal identification number
Pl.	place
p.m.	(*post meridiem*) afternoon
P.O.	post office
POW	prisoner of war
pp.	pages
Pres.	president
pro tem	(*pro tempore*) temporarily or for the time being
Prof.	professor
P.S.	(*post scriptum*) postscript
PST	Pacific standard time
qt	quart
qtr.	quarter
rad	radian
RAM	random access memory
R&D	research and development
Rd.	road

Common Abbreviations

Rev.	Reverend
RFD	Rural Free Delivery
R.N.	Registered Nurse
RR	railroad
R.S.V.P.	please answer
S.	south
S&L	savings and loan
s.d.	(*sine die*) without date
S.E.	southeast
SOP	standard operating procedure
SOS	Save Our Ship (signal for help)
Sq.	square
Sr.	senior
St.	saint or street
STP	standard temperature and pressure
Supt.	superintendent
S.W.	southwest
tbsp.	tablespoon
Ter.	terrace
tsp.	teaspoon
TV	television
UHF	ultra high frequency
UN	United Nations
univ.	university
USIA	United States Information Agency

8

Common Abbreviations	VAT	value-added tax
	VCR	videocassette recorder
	VHF	very high frequency
	VIP	very important person
	viz.	(*videlicet*) namely
	vol.	volume
	vs.	(*versus*) against
	w	watt
	W.	west
	WHO	World Health Organization
	wk	week
	wt.	weight
	x	unknown quantity
	xl	extra large
	yd	yard
	YMCA	Young Men's Christian Association
	YMHA	Young Men's Hebrew Association
	yr	year
	YTD	year to date
	YWCA	Young Women's Christian Association
	Zip Code	Zone Improvement Plan Code

ACRONYMS

Acronyms are abbreviations that are pronounced as words. They're formed by taking the first letter or letters of each word in a name or phrase. UNICEF, for example, is an acronym for United Nations International Children's Emergency Fund. Some acronyms have become so widely used they've become words in and of themselves. SONAR, which stands for SOund NAvigation Ranging, is an example.

Acronyms have become very popular in this century and are acceptable in formal writing for the same reason that abbreviations have gained acceptance—they prevent the repetition of long words and phrases. Even if the acronym is universally known, however, you should spell the name in full the first time you use it. There is often someone who has yet to learn that NOW stands for National Organization for Women even though that person may be familiar with the activities of NOW.

8

Amtrak	AMerican TRAcK
AIDS	Acquired Immune Deficiency Syndrome
ARAMCO	ARrabian AMerican oil COmpany
BIT	Binary DigiT
CORE	Congress Of Racial Equality
NOW	National Organization for Women
radar	RAdio Detecting And Ranging
SALT	Strategic Arms Limitation Treaty
sonar	SOund NAvigation Ranging
UNICEF	United Nations International Children's Emergency Fund
ZIP	Zone Improvement Plan

NUMBERS

The conventions for spelling out *numbers* as words or using figures vary from one kind of writing to another. Technical writers use figures more than anyone else. In fact, the technical difficulty of a piece of writing can almost be measured by the number of figures it contains. The general rule for numbers, however, is to spell out small numbers (those under 10) and to use figures for larger numbers, except when the number reads more easily if the word is used (a million). The important thing is to be consistent.

Here are some guidelines to follow when trying to decide whether to use the word for a number or the figure:

- Spell out numbers that begin a sentence.

    <u>Twenty-five</u> years ago, he flew for the first time.

    If the number that begins the sentence is very large, rewrite the sentence.

    He's flown <u>436</u> times since then.

- Spell out approximations of numbers that are used for effect rather than for accuracy.

    The boss told him <u>a million</u> times to keep his desk clean.

- Spell out the small numbers in street addresses.

    She lived at 2321 <u>Fourth</u> Avenue.

- Use figures for numbers containing fractions and ratios.

    Submit your report on <u>8 1/2</u> by 11-inch paper.

    The team is favored to win by <u>2-to-1</u> odds.

- Use figures for percentages and numbers containing decimal points.

    She's completed about <u>75</u> percent of the work.

    The sales tax here is <u>5.6</u> percent.

Note that in tables, figures, and charts, it's acceptable to use the percent symbol. In text, however, spell out the word *percent*.

- Use figures for dates.

    The war started on the 14th of August.

    The war started on 14 August 1914.

    The war started on August 14th, 1914.

    The war started on August 14, 1914.

- Use the letter *s* to form the plural of a figure.

    The 1970s were a difficult time for him.

    Again, rules vary about whether to use an apostrophe before the *s*. Use consistently whichever style you choose.

- Use figures to number lists:

    1. French   (1) French

    2. Spanish   (2) Spanish

    3. German   (3) German

- Combine figures and words for large, round numbers.

    The Knicks have over $35 million invested in him.

- Combine figures and words to distinguish one set of numbers from another set in a single sentence.

    You will need two 3-inch nails.

- Use figures for a.m. and p.m., but spell out the number before *o'clock*.

    He will arrive at ten o'clock.

    She will arrive at 9:30 a.m.

- Use figures to emphasize ages.

    At 24, he was the youngest person to be elected to the city council.

8

When Form is a Question

GLOSSARY

A *glossary* is a list of words and their definitions. It's placed at the end of any written work containing words that the general reader may not know.

Here's what a glossary may look like:

ACRONYM. A word formed from the first letter or first few letters of a group of words. AID, for example, is an acronym for Agency for International Development, while AIDS is an acronym for Acquired Immune Deficiency Syndrome.

ACTIVE VOICE. See VOICE.

ADJECTIVE. A word that describes or limits a noun or pronoun.

FOOTNOTES

Footnotes are used:

- To cite sources of information.
- To provide information of secondary importance to the text.
- To provide the reader with additional opinions.
- To refer the reader to other pages in the text.

Footnotes acknowledge information that comes from other sources. They should be numbered consecutively beginning with the number 1. Although they used to appear at the foot of the pages on which the references were made (hence, *foot*notes), they are now commonly placed at the end of a report or proposal, where they used to be called *endnotes* but are now called footnotes.

The footnote should include the author's full name, the title of the publication cited, the facts of the publication, and the page number from which the reference comes. Do not, however, repeat information in the text. If, for example, you've mentioned the author's name in the text, your footnote will begin with the title of the publication.

Different disciplines have different formats for footnotes. If your company doesn't require a specific form, the one presented here will almost certainly be acceptable.

- For books:

With one author:

H. W. Fowler, *Modern English Usage* (New York: Oxford University Press, 1985), p. 14.

With more than one author:

Jerry Brown and Denise Dudley. *The Supervisor's Guide* (Mission, KS: SkillPath Publications, 1989), p. 26.

- For magazine articles:

   Hennig Cohen, "Why Isn't Melville for the Masses?" *Saturday Review*, August 16, 1969, pp. 19-21.

- For newspaper articles:

   Irving Howe, "James Baldwin: At Ease in Apocalypse," *The New York Times*, October 10, 1976, Sec. 1, p. 37, col. 1.

BIBLIOGRAPHIES

The *bibliography* is a list of references and comes at the end of a report or proposal. The bibliography is an alphabetical listing of all the works cited in your footnotes, but it can and often should include all the works you consulted in preparing your report or proposal.

Unlike footnotes, which don't require a page of their own, the bibliography does. This separate page or pages should be placed after the footnotes in your text.

Bibliographies repeat information cited in a footnote but the format is different.

- For books:

   With one author:

   Frye, Northrop. *Anatomy of Criticism: Four Essays*. Princeton, NJ: Princeton University Press, 1957.

   With more than one author:

   Brown, Jerry, and Denise Dudley. *The Supervisor's Guide*. Mission, KS: SkillPath Publications, 1989.

   With no author:

   The New Lexicon Webster's Dictionary of the English Language. New York, NY: Lexicon Publications, Inc., 1990.

9

- For magazine articles:

    Ramsey, Jarold W. "The Wife Who Goes Like a Man, Comes Back as a Hero: The Art of Two Oregon Indian Narratives." *PMLA*, 92 (1977), pp. 9-18.

- For newspaper articles:

    Brody, Jane E. "Multiple Cancers Termed on Increase." *The New York Times*. October 10, 1976, Sec. 1, p. 37, col. 1.

INDEXES

Indexes list, in alphabetical order, the subjects contained in a written work. Next to each subject is the page number where that particular subject is discussed. The longer any document (more than 50 pages, for example), the more helpful an index becomes.

Indexes range from the simple to the complicated, but the best indexes are those that cater best to the needs of their readers.

Placed in its own section after the footnotes and bibliography, the index should look something like this:

Abbreviations

avoiding, 121, 122

for titles in letters, 188

in name and address in letters, 185, 186

Abstract of report or proposal, 223-224

Accuracy, rewriting and, 51

Acronyms, avoiding, 121, 122

Active voice, advantages over passive voice, 55, 114-115.

In general, avoid entries that just contain several page numbers. You're not doing your readers any favor by asking them to look up 10 pages to find the information needed. In these cases, break the entry into several subdivisions under the main entry.

CHARTS, GRAPHS, AND ILLUSTRATIONS

At one time, these words had different meanings. Now the meanings have become so blurred that a *chart* can mean a *graph*, both can be considered *illustrations*, and all three could be grouped under the popular heading *visual aids*. Regardless of what they're called, they have one function: to communicate quickly and effectively an important idea to readers.

There are many ways to arrange visuals, but the most effective visuals:

- Are easy to locate.

- Are easy to read.

- Are labeled clearly.

- Are placed in the text where they will most help the reader.

- Tell the reader what is important in each graphic.

- Feature an explanatory sentence or short paragraph under each graphic to help the reader interpret it.

Often the most creative visuals are found in the newspaper *USA Today*. Consult any issue for examples of how you might improve the effectiveness of any report or proposal.

9

LISTS

Lists aren't considered visual aids, but they could be. Their single great advantage is that they draw the reader's eyes right into the page. Compare the densely written paragraph on the left with its updated rewrite on the right, and notice how before reading a single word, your eyes gravitate to the statement on the right.

The Privacy Act of 1974 provides that each Federal Agency inform individuals, whom it asks to supply information, of the authority for the solicitation of the information and whether disclosure of such information is mandatory or voluntary; the principle purpose or purposes for which the information is to be used; the routine uses which may be made of the information; and the effects on the individual of not providing the requested information.

The Privacy Act of 1974 says that each Federal Agency that asks you for information must tell you the following:

1. Its legal right to ask for the information and whether the law says you must give it

2. What purpose the agency has in asking for it, and how the information may be used

3. What could happen if you do not give it

Did you notice that the paragraph on the left is all one sentence? That's a lot to ask of any reader.

Here are some mechanical tips to follow when using lists:

- Designate each item with a number followed by a period or with a graphic device such as a bullet.

- Capitalize the first letter of the first word of each item.

- End each item with a period only if the item grammatically completes the thought of the phrase that introduces it; otherwise, no punctuation is necessary.

- End the introductory phrase with a colon.

- Begin each item on a separate line.

HEADINGS

Headings tell the reader what a memo, letter, report, or proposal is about. In many ways, a heading is like a title: it tells the reader what is important about what is to come. It gives the reader the opportunity to skim a document and also to quickly refresh his or her memory after reading it.

Like lists, headings draw the reader's eyes to the page and help make the text easier to comprehend. Headings can appear in UPPERCASE, *italics*, or any way you think is most effective.

Write It Right! A Guide for Clear and Correct Writing provides excellent examples on every page of how headings can be used. Take your pick. The important thing is, once you've chosen the style and format that best suits your needs, be consistent. If you decide to begin your first heading with a verb, try to make the headings that follow also begin with verbs. If your first heading is ALL IN CAPITAL LETTERS, don't place the next heading in *italics*, unless it's a subheading. But, in general, all headings that represent the same level of importance should be styled the same.

9

10

Writing That Means Business

W e live in an age of increasing dehumanization. For this reason, people are looking for human contacts. Business people who provide these contacts are going to establish the kinds of human relationships that lead to success.

The fastest, easiest, most effective way to come across as a human being in our memos, letters, reports, and proposals is to write in our own natural voices. To be the same person on paper that our clients and colleagues talk to on the telephone.

Phrases such as "prioritized evaluation procedures" only blur our messages and dull our readers.

MEMOS

Memos, an abbreviation for *memoranda* or *memorandums,* are notes or letters written to people within your organization. They vary in length and form depending on the purpose of the memo and the company you work for. Because they're intended for an internal audience, however, they tend to be less formal than business letters.

Before writing any memo ask yourself:

- *Who am I writing to?* Not merely your reader's name, but what position does he or she hold in the company? How does my reader think? Feel? Act? What motivates my reader? What are my reader's biases? The more we know about our readers, the more ways we have of influencing them.

- *What do I want to say?* State in specific terms what you want the reader to do, when you want it done, and, if possible, what you can do for the reader if your request is completed on time.

After writing any memo ask yourself:

- Have I opened with the most important idea?

- Have I organized the rest of my thoughts in a logical progression?

- Have I eliminated any unnecessary words?

Although memo formats vary from one organization to another, most memos have a *heading,* a *body,* and a *signature.*

- *The heading:*

    To:

    From:

    Subject:

    Date:

- *The body.* Some memos are printed; others are handwritten. Some paragraphs of some memos are indented; others are presented in block form. It all depends on the nature of the memo and the requirements of your company.

- *The signature.* Even though the author's name appears after "From:" in the memo's heading, many writers sign their name below the final line of the text. The signature, the most personal part of any memo, is almost always more effective when it is handwritten.

LETTERS

Effective letters do more than convey information; they establish relationships. Here are eight things you can do to improve the quality of every letter you write:

- *Keep it short.* Busy people don't have time to read long-winded letters.

- *Call the person you're writing to by name.* Try not to write a "Dear Sir or Madam" letter. Telephone the company you're writing to, get the name of a specific person, and be sure to spell it correctly. Letters written to specific people are answered faster and more effectively than letters written to whoever happens to open the mail.

- *Avoid stale openings and closings.* Letters that begin "In reference to your letter of September 19th, I hereby wish to inform you that . . ." cause a glaze to move across your reader's eyes. Pretend your reader is sitting right in front of you at your desk. Would you say "Enclosed herewith please find . . ." or "Here's the information you asked for . . ."? Whatever you would say to that person sitting right in front of you, say it the same way in your letter.

- *Analyze what you've written from the reader's point of view.* Ask yourself, "What's in this for the reader?" "Why should my reader agree with me?" Try to see everything from how the reader will respond.

10

- *Use positive-sounding words.* Words like *questionable* and *misinformed* make our readers want to distance themselves from us. Words such as *agreeable* and *advantage* bring them closer to our messages.

- *Be specific.* Say exactly what you want the reader to do and when you want the reader to do it—two simple things that improve the effectiveness of every letter we write.

- *Make sure there are no mistakes.* If your letters contain mistakes, your readers are going to think you're either ignorant or careless. To avoid giving either of these impressions, make every letter as close to perfect as you can possibly get it.

- *Sign your name so people can read it.* And don't be afraid to sign it big. That shows you're important.

Letter formats vary from company to company, but most formats have these characteristics in common:

- *The date.*

    19 September 1993

    August 4, 1993

- *The inside address.* The inside address usually includes:

    The addressee's title: Ms. Joan Doe

    The addressee's company: United Bank

    The company's address: 45 Federal St.

    The company's city, state, and ZIP code: Hull, MA 02115

Note: Though most people can be addressed as *Mr.* or *Ms.*, the titles of some people require a special address.

Title:	*Address:*	*Salutation:*
Admiral	Admiral John Jones	Dear Admiral Jones:
Ambassador	The Honorable John Jones	Dear Mr. Ambassador:

Archbishop	The Most Reverend John Jones	Dear Archbishop Jones:
Archdeacon	The Venerable John Jones	Venerable Sir:
Attorney General	The Honorable John Jones	Dear Mr. Jones:
Bishop	The Most Reverend John Jones	Dear Bishop Jones:
Brother	Brother Andrew Jones	Dear Brother Andrew:
Cabinet Officer	The Honorable John Jones	Dear Mr. Secretary:
Cardinal	His Eminence, Cardinal John Jones	Your Eminence:
Chancellor	Dr. John Jones	Dear Dr. Jones:
Chaplain	Chaplain	Dear Chaplain Jones:
Chief Justice	The Chief Justice	Dear Mr. Chief Justice:
City Council	The City Council	Honorable Sirs:
Convent Superior	Reverend Mother Mary Jones	Dear Reverend Mother:
General	General Anne Jones	Dear General Jones:
Governor	The Honorable Anne Jones	Dear Governor Jones:
Judge	The Honorable John Jones	Dear Judge Jones:
Mayor	The Honorable Anne Jones	Dear Mayor Jones:
Minister	The Reverend John Jones	Dear Reverend Jones:
Monsignor	The Right Reverend Monsignor Jones	Dear Monsignor Jones:
The Pope	His Holiness Pope John Paul II	Your Holiness:
President	The President	Dear Mr. President:
Priest	The Reverend Paul Jones	Dear Father Jones:
Principal	Dr., Mr., Ms. (first name) Jones	Dear Dr., Mr., Ms. Jones:
Rabbi	Rabbi John Jones	Dear Rabbi Jones:
Rector	The Very Reverend	Dear Rev. Jones:
Senator	The Honorable John Jones	Dear Senator Jones:
Sister	Sister Mary Jones	Dear Sister Mary:

10

- *The salutation.* If you don't know the name of the person you're writing to, "Dear Sir or Madam:" is the standard form of address. "To Whom It May Concern:" is considered dated, and "Dear Sir:" or "Gentlemen:" almost guarantees that your letter will wind up in the wastepaper basket. If "Dear Sir or Madam:" doesn't appeal to you, consider:

  Dear Colleagues:

  Dear Friends:

  Dear Members of the Search Committee:

  Dear Customer Service Representative:

  Here are some standard forms of salutation for when you do know the addressee's name:

  Dear Mr. Jones:

  Dear Ms. Jones:

  Dear Jane:

  Dear Jane Jones:

  Dear Dr. Jones:

  Dear Prof. Jones:

  Dear President Jones:

  Note that in business correspondence a colon follows the addressee's name.

- *The subject line.* Although not universally used, subject lines are appearing in more and more business correspondence. They call attention to what's important in the letter and can appear either above or below the salutation. Most formats place it above.

- *The body.* The body of most letters is single spaced, and indentations depend on the company's chosen format. Most business writers try to keep their letters to one page.

- *The complimentary closing.* Where the closing appears varies according to the format used by individual companies. In most formal, but not stuffy letters, the common closing is:

  Sincerely,

  Other closings include:

  Sincerely yours,

  Thank you,

  Yours truly,

  With best wishes,

  With best regards,

  Cordially,

- *The signature block.* The signature block begins with your handwritten name. A formal letter carries your full name, while a more casual business letter may present just your first name.

  Under your signature, however, your full name is always printed, often followed by your title.

  Sincerely,

  Jane Jones
  Sales Manager

  If your company's name and address do not appear at the top of the stationery you're using, list them under your title. If you're writing a personal letter to a company, list your address under your printed name.

10

If you have not mentioned your telephone number in the body of your letter, you may wish to include it under your address.

Sincerely,

Jane Jones
25 North Pleasant St.
Amherst, MA 01059
413-256-7985

REPORTS AND PROPOSALS

There are as many different formats for reports and proposals as there are professions, but there are some things most formal reports and proposals have in common:

- *A title page.* The title page can include:

    The title of the document.

    The author's name.

    The date of submission.

    The organization's name.

- *A preface or foreword.* This can include:

    References to other reports on the same subject.

    Reasons why the report was written.

    Acknowledgment of anyone who helped with the report.

- *A table of contents*. This outline of the report should help the reader locate particular sections in the report or proposal. It can also include subheadings.

- *A body*. The important thing here is to be as clear and as concise as possible. The usual progression is to argue from the general to the particular or from fact to conclusion, but here are some other things to keep in mind:

Don't talk down to your readers.

Anticipate your readers' objections.

Consider beginning with points everyone can agree on.

10

- *A conclusion.* If you are writing a report, your conclusion should grow out of information already stated in your report and should be stated with some conviction. A proposal should contain these same qualities, but it should also argue for the changes you propose and how these changes will benefit your company.

- *A bibliography.* The bibliography lists the books and articles you consulted in preparing to write your report or proposal.

Reports and proposals also sometimes contain:

- *A cover.* Covers often appear on reports and proposals to protect them from the effects of widespread distribution. The cover should contain roughly the same information that appears on the title page.

- *A letter of transmittal.* The letter of transmittal introduces the report or proposal. It might mention how the need for the report or proposal was brought to your attention, some of the problems you had in writing, how your study might relate to previous reports or proposals, and what your document excludes.

- *An abstract.* Usually no longer than one page in length and placed before the body, the abstract briefly describes the content of the report or proposal.

- *A summary.* Usually placed after the body and before the conclusion, the summary restates in a brief form the major points of the body.

- *An appendix.* Usually appearing before the bibliography, the appendix contains secondary but important information that was too lengthy to be included in the body of the report or proposal.

Use as many different appendixes as there are kinds of information:

Appendix A: Clichés

Appendix B: Redundancies

Appendix C: Jargon

CHAPTER 11

A Final Word on Writing

Writing is a skill just like swinging a baseball bat or staying afloat in water. It may take a lot of time and effort to become a pro at it, but all native speakers of English have the ability to be competent, to write in the same clear, easy-to-understand prose that they speak.

Write as closely as possible to the way you speak to clients on the telephone—that's your natural voice maintaining a professional tone—and proofread out loud. Do these two things and you'll eliminate all but a few of your common spelling, punctuation, and grammatical errors.

And how do you identify and correct those few errors you repeat over and over again? Give something you've written of about 150 words to someone else to correct. When you get the corrected document back, make a list of your mistakes.

Then give that same person another piece of writing of 150 words. When you get the document back, add to your list of mistakes. Only just don't list the new mistakes; list every single mistake every single time. After about five or six documents, you'll notice a pattern developing.

Once you've identified from the pattern the two or three mistakes you're most likely to make, find out how to correct your mistakes in *Write it Right!* Then, in the future, all you have to do is:

Write in your own voice.

Proofread aloud.

**Look out for those two or three
mistakes you're most likely to make.**

Do these three things and it will be very rare for a spelling, punctuation, or grammatical error to slip by you ever again.

The Ten Commandments of Business Writing Style

   I. Write more like you talk.
   II. Use short, clear words.
   III. Aim for an average of 10 to 12 words per sentence.
   IV. Use active voice verbs as often as possible.
   V. Be positive and personal.
   VI. Be consistent with whatever style you choose.
   VII. Avoid clichés and jargon.
   VIII. Harness the power of concrete words and specific terms.
   IX. Eliminate sexist and biased language—both conscious AND unconscious.
   X. Aim to be yourself.

ACRONYM. A word formed from the first letter or first few letters of a group of words. AID, for example, is an acronym for <u>A</u>gency for <u>I</u>nternational <u>D</u>evelopment, while AIDS is an acronym for <u>A</u>cquired <u>I</u>mmune <u>D</u>eficiency <u>S</u>yndrome.

ACTIVE VOICE. Active voice is when the subject of the sentence is doing the action: <u>John hit the ball.</u>

Tip: Almost always, active voice is shorter, clearer, simpler, more direct, and easier to understand than passive voice.

ADJECTIVE. A word that describes or limits a noun or pronoun: Mary purchased a <u>large</u> bag.

Tip: Whenever possible, replace your adjective with a specific detail or an example of what you mean by that adjective. Instead of saying "<u>substantial</u> savings," say, "You put $10 in this account for the next six months, and you can have $275 for your July vacation."

ADVERB. A word that modifies a verb, adjective, or another adverb: I want you <u>here</u> in the morning.

Tip: As with adjectives, try to replace adverbs with a specific detail. Instead of "I'll call you <u>soon</u>," try "I'll call you <u>next Tuesday at ten o'clock.</u>"

AGREEMENT. One of the ways words relate to each other. Subjects and predicates should agree in number and person: The <u>newspaper</u> with the best reporters <u>does</u> the best job. Pronouns and the words they take the place of should agree in number, person, and gender: Each <u>director</u> turned in <u>his or her</u> recommendation.

ANTECEDENT. The word or words a pronoun or adjective refers to. In the sentence "<u>Larry</u> thinks <u>he</u> is Lee Iacocca," *Larry* is the antecedent of *he.*

CLAUSE. A group of words containing a subject and a predicate. An *independent clause* is a complete sentence: <u>Larry thinks he is Lee Iacocca.</u> A *dependent clause* has a subject and a predicate but cannot stand alone as a sentence: <u>Because Larry saved the company.</u>

COLLECTIVE NOUN. A noun that refers to a group of persons or things but is considered singular because the group acts as one: The <u>committee</u> met.

COMMA SPLICE. A comma splice occurs when two independent clauses are joined with a comma instead of a comma and a conjunction: John hit it, Mary caught it.

COMPLEX SENTENCE. A complex sentence contains an independent clause and a dependent clause: <u>When the telephone rang</u> (dependent clause), <u>the door also opened</u> (independent clause).

COMPOUND SENTENCE. A compound sentence contains two independent clauses: <u>The telephone rang,</u> and <u>the door opened at the same time.</u>

CONJUNCTION. A word used to connect other words: John <u>and</u> Mary showed up ahead of time.

CONTRACTION. A word that has been shortened by taking out one or more letters and replacing them with an apostrophe: Jill <u>won't</u> be able to make the meeting.

> Tip: We speak in contractions all the time. When we see them in print, we relax and allow ourselves to be drawn closer to the message. Contractions will not only draw your readers into your message, they'll also help you come across as sounding warmer and more personable. Avoid contractions, however, if the subject matter is serious or if you need to maintain a more formal relationship with your reader.

DANGLING MODIFIER. A modifier that has nothing to modify: <u>Having fixed the flat tire</u>, the car refused to start. Who fixed the flat tire? Who failed to start the car?

DEPENDENT CLAUSE. See **CLAUSE.**

DOUBLE NEGATIVE. Two negative words in the same clause: That teacher thought I <u>didn't</u> have <u>no</u> Ph.D.

GENDER. The classification of nouns according to whether they are <u>masculine</u>, <u>feminine</u>, or <u>neuter</u>.

    Tip: Avoid gender-specific language unless necessary.

INDEPENDENT CLAUSE. See **CLAUSE.**

INTERJECTION. A word injected into a sentence to show emotion. It usually is unrelated grammatically to the rest of the sentence: <u>Oh</u>, don't do that!

MISPLACED MODIFIER. A modifier that modifies the wrong word: Michael spent two weeks in bed <u>with</u> his medicine.

    Tip: Because understanding in English depends on word order rather than on word endings (as in French, Spanish, and Italian), try to keep your modifying words, phrases, and clauses as close as possible to the words they modify.

MODIFIER. A word, phrase, or clause that changes the meaning of a word, usually by limiting it or qualifying it in some way. Adverbs and adjectives are examples of modifiers. See **DANGLING MODIFIER** and **MISPLACED MODIFIER**.

NOUN. A noun is the name of a person, place, or thing.

    Tip: Readers focus on nouns because nouns are where the information is. If readers are going to notice an error, they are most likely going to find it in a noun.

NUMBER. The classification of nouns and pronouns as *singular* or *plural*. In matters of subject and verb agreement, singular nouns take singular verbs and plural nouns take plural verbs.

OBJECT. The noun or pronoun that follows a verb: Mary gave <u>the book</u> (object of a verb) to <u>John</u> (object of a preposition).

PARAGRAPH. A paragraph sets off a section of written material that focuses on a particular idea. Paragraphs can be one word long or, in the case of the final chapter of James Joyce's *Ulysses*, 55 pages. Or more.

Tip: Varying the length of your paragraphs is an effective and subtle way to keep your reader engaged in your message.

PASSIVE VOICE. Passive voice is when the action is being done to the subject of a sentence: The ball <u>was hit</u> by John.

Tip: There's nothing wrong with passive voice, but more often than not, it is less clear and direct than active voice. Moreover, the extra words used to form passive voice slow the reader down.

PERSON. The way we distinguish the speaker or speakers: *I* and *we*, for example, are first person; *you* is second person; *they* is third person.

Tip: It's acceptable now in business letters to write in the first person.

PHRASE. A group of grammatically related words that do not contain both a subject and a predicate: <u>on his desk</u>.

Tip: Phrases can stand alone as sentences if you use them effectively: So where did he finally find his keys? <u>On his desk</u>.

PREDICATE. The verb that tells us what the subject of the sentence is doing: Leslie <u>placed</u> it on his desk.

Tip: Verbs are action words. They make writing come alive.

PREFIX. A group of letters that, while not a word by themselves, can be added to the beginning of a word to change that word's meaning: <u>re</u>play, <u>un</u>necessary.

PREPOSITION. Usually a small word that connects a noun with some other word or words in a sentence: Leslie placed it <u>on</u> the desk.

Tip: It's usually more effective to write a natural-sounding sentence that ends with a preposition than to opt for a sentence that is grammatically correct but sounds awkward.

Natural-sounding: I'm the one you spoke <u>to</u>.

Awkward: I'm the one <u>to</u> whom you spoke.

PREPOSITIONAL PHRASE. The preposition together with its object forms a prepositional phrase: Leslie placed it <u>on the desk</u>.

PRONOUNS. A group of words that take the place of nouns so that the nouns don't have to be repeated: Mike finished <u>his</u> proposal and handed <u>it</u> to <u>her</u>.

Tip: Pronouns that indicate the possessive case don't require apostrophes: *yours, theirs, its, ours.*

SENTENCE. A complete thought containing both a subject and a predicate: <u>I want to see your proposal</u>.

SENTENCE FRAGMENT. An incomplete sentence that may contain a subject and a predicate but does not express a complete thought: <u>Because of the recent survey</u>. Sentence fragments can stand alone, however, if used effectively: <u>How do I know this</u>? <u>Because of the recent survey</u>.

SPLIT INFINITIVE. The combination of the word *to* and a verb. To split an infinitive, traditionally considered grammatically incorrect, is to place a word or words between the *to* and the verb that follows it: to <u>eagerly</u> agree. Despite tradition, split infinitives have become increasingly popular, and to rearrange many would make the resulting grammatically correct sentences sound awkward: You're going <u>to enjoy wholeheartedly</u> that movie.

SUBJECT. The noun in a sentence that is doing the action or is being acted upon. In the sentence "<u>John</u> hit the ball," *John* is doing the action. In "The <u>ball</u> was hit by John," the *ball* is being acted upon.

SUBORDINATION. When one or more clauses in a sentence are grammatically dependent on some other word or words: <u>After he took the file from the cabinet</u>, he realized he didn't need it.

SUFFIX. A group of letters that, while not words, can be added to the ends of words to change their meaning or use: joy<u>ful</u>, entire<u>ly</u>.

SYNTAX. The way we arrange our words to form phrases, clauses, and sentences.

TENSE. The way time is described by a verb: It <u>happens</u> (present tense); it <u>happened</u> (past tense); it <u>will happen</u> (future tense).

Tip: There's nothing wrong with changing tenses within a letter or a paragraph. If, however, you think a certain change in tense may confuse your reader, begin a new paragraph when you're ready to change tense. The new paragraph will alert your reader that something new is taking place.

VERB. A word that expresses action (Mary <u>pulled</u>) or state of being (Mary <u>is</u>).

VOICE. Voice tells us how a verb relates to its subject. See **ACTIVE VOICE** and **PASSIVE VOICE** for the two ways verbs indicate action.

Dictionary

Webster's New World Dictionary of American English, Third College Edition (Merriam-Webster)

Word Books

Laird, Charlton, *Webster's New World Thesaurus* (Simon & Schuster)

Modern Guide to Synonyms and Related Words (Funk & Wagnalls)

Morse-Cluley, Elizabeth, and Richard Read, *Webster's New World Power Vocabulary* (Simon & Schuster)

The New Webster's Desk Reference Library (Lexicon Publications)

Oxford Dictionary of Quotations (Oxford University Press)

Webster's New World Misspellers Dictionary (Simon & Schuster)

Webster's New World Thesaurus (Merriam-Webster)

Style Guides

Bacon, Terry R. and Lawrence H. Freeman, *Shipley Associates Style Guide—Writing in the World of Work* (Shipley Associates)

Eckersley-Johnson, Anna L., *Webster's Secretarial Handbook* (Merriam-Webster)

Elements of Style (McGraw-Hill)

Sabin, William A., *The Gregg Reference Manual* (McGraw-Hill)

Strunk, William, and E.B. White, *The Elements of Style* (Macmillan)

Usage Guide

Modern English Usage (Oxford University Press)

Books on Writing

Andersen, Richard, *Writing That Works* (McGraw-Hill)

Brock, Susan L., *Better Business Writing* (Crisp Publications)

Flesch, Rudolph, *How to Write, Speak and Think More Effectively* (Harper & Row)

Hinis, Helene, *Power Write* (SkillPath Publications)

Joseph, Albert, *Executive Guide to Grammar* (International Writing Institute)

Reid, Jr., James M., and Anne Silleck, *Better Business Letters* (Addison-Wesley)

Swenson, Jack, *Writing Fitness* (Crisp Publications)

Audiocassettes

Booher, Dianna, *Write to the Point* (Nightingale-Conant)

Koehnline, William A., *Winning with Words* (Nightingale-Conant)

Poley, Michelle Fairfield, *Powerful Proofreading and Editing Skills* (SkillPath Publications)

BIBLIOGRAPHY

Andersen, Richard. *Writing That Works: A Practical Guide for Business and Creative People.* New York: McGraw-Hill, 1989.

Brock, Susan L. *Better Business Writing.* Los Altos, CA: Crisp, 1987.

Corbett, Edward. *The Little English Handbook: Choices and Conventions.* Glenview, IL: Scott, Foresman, 1984.

Elbow, Peter. *Writing Without Teachers.* New York: Oxford University Press, 1973.

Freeman, Lawrence, and Terry Bacon. *Style Guide.* Bountiful, UT: Shipley Associates, 1990.

Hall, Donald. *Writing Well.* Boston: Little, Brown, 1976.

Hinis, Helene. *Power Write! A Practical Guide to Words That Work.* Mission, KS: SkillPath, 1989.

Miller, Casey, and Kate Swift. *The Handbook of Nonsexist Writing for Writers, Editors, and Speakers.* New York: Barnes and Noble, 1980.

Millward, Celia. *Handbook for Writers.* New York: Holt, Rinehart and Winston, 1980.

Strunk, William Jr., and E. B. White. *The Elements of Style.* New York: Macmillan, 1959.

Swenson, Jack. *The Building Blocks of Business Writing.* Los Altos, CA: Crisp, 1991.

Zinsser, William. *On Writing Well.* New York: Harper & Row, 1976.

INDEX

162

INDEX

INDEX